Northern Lights, Southern Nights:
A Memoir of Writing Parents

T0159030

"The constantly changing forms and patterns of the masses of light and the flow of colors bewilder the eye, forcing it to change focus again and again, encouraging the mind to wander, stimulating the imagination, and multiplying thought. For generations, the northern lights have been a source of wonder, mystery and inspiration."

Asgeir Brekke, assistant professor of physics at the
University of Tromso, Norway, describing the aurora borealis.

"It has been two or three years since I have seen the northern lights. Where have they gone? I miss them. They always make my heart leap and something of primitive fear comes over me. We never entirely lose our caveman memories."

Susan Frawley Eisele

"I can only say that in each story that I write, I have an aim: to evoke either the spirit of tragedy, or the spirit of happiness. It is mostly tragedy to which I devote myself, because this spirit is nearer to surface, is far more common; and because, I suppose, I have seen so much of it in the last ten or fifteen years here in the Middle West."

Albert Eisele

"You can't go back home to your family, back home to your childhood . . . back home to a young man's dreams of glory and of fame . . . back home to places in the country, back home to the old forms and systems of things which once seemed everlasting but which are changing all the time—back home to the escapes of Time and Memory."

Thomas Wolfe, You Can't Go Home Again

Northern Lights, Southern Nights

A Memoir of Writing Parents

by

Albert Eisele

P*

Polaris Publications
St. Cloud, Minnesota

Dedicated
to
Moira, Kitty, and Anne

ISBN 978-0-87839-831-7

Second Printing January 2015

Published by Polaris Publications
an imprint of
North Star Press of St. Cloud, Inc.
P.O. Box 451
St. Cloud, Minnesota 56302

northstarpress.com

Table of Contents

Prologue

Albert and Susan

MY PARENTS CAME from backgrounds so different that only fate and their mutual passion for writing could have brought them together.

My father was an Iowa farm boy, the second of six children of German immigrants. Born in 1896 in Illinois, he moved with his family in 1902 to a farm in northern Iowa, where his formal education ended in the eighth grade in a school run by Catholic nuns. Yet, even as he had to forego high school and college because he was needed to help run the family farm, he had an insatiable hunger for learning and an innate talent for writing, recognized and encouraged by the nuns. Determined to become a published writer, he persisted despite years of disappointment and rejection, and by the time of his death in 1951, had won widespread acclaim in the Catholic literary community for his short stories and poems.

My mother was a daughter of the South. Born in 1897 on South Carolina's Atlantic seacoast, she was the oldest of ten children of Irish and Swiss immigrants. In 1905, she moved with her family to Newport in the scenic Smoky Mountains of East Tennessee. After high school, she attended an avant-garde women's academy run by a social activist Catholic priest near Asheville, North Carolina, then attended the Knoxville Business College and the Knoxville College of Law while working as a reporter for her local newspaper. She was one of the first women in Tennessee to earn a law degree, but decided against practicing law and worked as an office manager while writing and reporting for several Tennessee newspapers and contributing to a Catholic newspaper in Dubuque, Iowa. Among the stories she covered was the historic Scopes "monkey trial" in Dayton, Tennessee, in 1925.

Her work for the Iowa newspaper led to her meeting my father, who began contributing to the same publication in 1920. After he criticized several of her columns, including one about the differences between men and women, they began a correspondence that blossomed into a long-distance romance, and in 1926, he traveled from Iowa to Tennessee to meet her. I have a photograph from that visit that I assume she took; he is sitting on a mountainside, a handsome Gary Cooper look-alike in a leather jacket. She was a lovely Southern belle, and it's no wonder they fell in love. They were married two years later in Newport, despite their parents' objections. "My mother didn't want me to marry an Iowa farmer because she thought I'd work too hard," she recalled. "His mother didn't want him to marry me because she thought Southern girls were too lazy." They began their life together on a 160-acre farm that his father bought near Blue Earth in southern Minnesota, and had six children, three of whom died in infancy. I was their last child, born in 1936. My mother, who died in 1984, said her honeyed Southern accent amused the local townspeople, who complained they couldn't understand her.

After their marriage in 1928, they continued to write, often early in the morning or late at night by the light of kerosene lanterns after finishing their farm chores and housework. My father wrote short stories and poems while my mother began writing unsigned commentary for the Blue Earth weekly newspaper in 1932 and a column for a daily newspaper in nearby Fairmont in 1933. The latter, called "With a Penny Pencil," brought her national attention in 1936 when she was named the nation's outstanding rural newspaper correspondent for a column she wrote on threshing grain. (She learned of the award, which included a trip to New York and Washington, on June 28, the day I was born.) Together, they also wrote a weekly farm and home column called "Countryside" in the *Blue Earth Post*, which was syndicated and appeared in some thirty Midwestern newspapers, while my father wrote a separate column for the Blue Earth paper called "The Post Chaise" and for *The Wanderer*, a Catholic newspaper in St. Paul. My mother also wrote a column for *The Witness*, a Catholic magazine in Dubuque, Iowa, from 1949 to 1981, and collaborated with a friend, Florence Hynes Willette, on a column in the Knights of Columbus magazine, *Columbia*, for many years.

But my father's consuming interest was writing short stories and poems that described life in rural America. Undaunted by years of rejections, he published his first poem in *Spirit* magazine in 1935 and his first short story in *The Catholic World* two years later, followed by a dozen poems and eighty short stories in other Catholic literary journals and rural life magazines before his death in 1951. He wrote more than forty stories that were rejected and nearly seventy more that were unpublished, along with an unpublished novel. Sev-

Albert watches with a critical eye as Susan writes one of her columns.

eral of his short stories appeared in anthologies of prominent Catholic writers, alongside such luminaries as Thomas Merton, Jacques Maritain, G.K. Chesterton, Georges Bernanos, J.F. Powers, and Dorothy Day, who came to our farm to meet him during a trip to Minnesota in 1946.

***

On the evening of September 1, 1951, my father sat at the desk in his room at the Hotel Campbell next to the Mayo Clinic in Rochester, Minnesota, and wrote to his four sisters and brother. I found a copy of his letter to his youngest sister, Mary Bode, and her husband, Herman, in Corwith, Iowa. "Dear Herman and Mary," he wrote in pencil in an even hand on hotel stationery. "Well, what would you say if I told you I had about a year to live? I wish I was joking, but I am not. Since Friday I have been going through the Clinic, and today they told me I had cancer of the right kidney. It is too far gone to cut out. I never had any pains in the back or kidneys, and this thing crept up on me like a thief in the night. Sorry to have to write you bad news, but we might as well face the truth." He added, "Pray for me," and signed it, "Albert."

He was fifty-five years old and had never had any major health problems. But his prediction that he had about a year to live soon proved too optimistic. Two-and-a-half months later, on November 14, he died in a hospital in Blue Earth. I was fifteen, a freshman in high school and the youngest of three brothers and the only one still living at home. I don't recall how or when I learned of his fatal diagnosis, but I remember the emaciated figure who lay in a makeshift bed in our house that fall before he was moved to the Blue Earth hospital. The last time I saw him, he weakly waved a hand of greeting and asked how I was doing in school. "Work hard and be good to your mother," he said. I assured him I would. A few days later, the father of one of my classmates came to our school and informed me that my father had passed away.

My father's untimely death came just when he was gaining recognition in Catholic literary circles for his short stories depicting life in the rural Midwest. I had been aware of this, but it wasn't until I went through the vast collection of his personal papers and literary output many years later that it became clear that his contemporaries held him in high esteem. Only a few days before my father left for the Mayo Clinic, he received a letter from Bruce Bliven, editorial director of *The New Republic*, praising one of his short stories that had just appeared in the Jesuit magazine, *America*. "That was a touching little sketch of yours in *America* for August 18, and beautifully done," Bliven wrote. "My envious congratulations." A month earlier, James O'Gara, editor of the national Catholic monthly, *The Voice of St. Jude*, sent him a check for a story in the magazine's July issue, accompanied by the words, "I have almost discontinued short stories here because so many terrible ones come in. It was a real pleasure to be able to print a decent one." Long after my father's death, Fr. Harold Gardiner, literary editor of *America*, wrote my mother in 1956, "I always was most happy and eager when Albert's short stories appeared on my desk, and I think that over the years I accepted more of his work than of any other single contributor. He had a very warm and human touch and obviously knew and loved what he was writing about."

***

In December 1987, Mrs. Mary Bode died in a hospital in Mason City, Iowa, not far from her home in the small town of Wesley. Stricken by a heart attack at eighty-six, she was playing cards with friends, a cherished pastime since the death of her husband ten years earlier. She was the youngest of my father's five siblings, and my favorite aunt, and I didn't learn of her death until the day before her funeral. I called her home that evening, where family and friends were gathered for a wake, and spoke to two of her four children, cousins I hadn't seen for many years. I also spoke with another cousin, Clem Bisenius, whose widowed mother was now my father's only surviving sibling. Lydia Bisenius was in an assisted living home in the nearby town of Whittemore, not far from the farm where she and her two brothers and three sisters grew up.

My cousin said that one of his sons, the father of a future major league baseball pitcher, was compiling a family history, and asked if I could locate a short story about baseball that my father had written. His request sent me searching through the dusty attic of my home in Falls Church, Virginia, where I found a half dozen cardboard boxes labeled "Albert's and Susan's writings," which I and my brothers had gathered through the years, and I had collected with the vague notion of someday writing about my parents.

In one of them, I found the article, titled "The Baseball Suit," which appeared in *The Ave Maria* on June 23, 1945, along with a vast collection of his other published short stories and poems. In another box, I found more than 130 of his short stories and more than a hundred poems that weren't published—many accompanied by letters of rejection—as well as hundreds of newspaper columns he wrote over three decades. Another box yielded a handwritten journal he kept as he was dying of cancer in 1951 and several versions of an unpublished novel—whose central character ironically was a man dying of cancer. Other boxes yielded an equally large collection of my mother's writings, including hundreds of newspaper and magazine columns dating back to the early 1920s, along with extensive personal correspondence, newspaper clippings, photographs, and family history. Much of the material, especially that of my father's, came as a revelation to me.

***

In October 2012, I received an e-mail from the stepdaughter of my older brother Arnold, who lived in West Palm Beach, Florida, where he ran a pet store. She informed me that he had been taken to a hospital and diagnosed with terminal cancer and was not expected to live more than a few days. I knew he was ailing, having visited him a year earlier and talked and corresponded with him regularly. He was suffering from a variety of ailments, from heart disease to prostate cancer, and although he still drove to work from his nearby condo, was using a walker and had turned the business over to his stepson. But his stepdaughter informed me that his cancer had spread to his lungs and spine, and told me if I wanted to see him, I should come immediately. I flew to Florida the next day and spent his last hours with him. He was still lucid and told me, as he had in a letter a year earlier, how proud of me he was and how he hoped I would write a memoir of my parents. I promised him I would, and he died a few hours later.

When I returned home after my brother's death and examined the vast array of material representing my parents' collected writing, I realized it was not only a rich repository of family history, but a priceless archive that would allow me to reconstruct the lives of two remarkable people and gifted writers who happened to be my parents. It was an opportunity, indeed, an obligation and command, to keep my promise to a dying brother, and to embark on a journey of personal discovery by examining their lives through their writings. This, then, is their story, and to a lesser extent, mine as well.

Chapter One

Iowa Farm Boy

THERE WAS NO APPARENT REASON for my father's determination to become a writer, nothing in his family history or background that hinted of literary ambition. Born in Illinois in 1896, he moved with his family in 1902 to a farm near the small northern Iowa town of Whittemore, where he grew up with five siblings, none of whom went to college or aspired to be writers. He attended the Presentation Academy, a grade school at St. Michael's Catholic Church run by nuns who came from Dubuque in 1903.

He had only an eighth-grade education but dreamed of going to Marquette College in Milwaukee, but his father said he was needed at home, and his formal education ended at age fourteen. He had natural athletic ability, starring on the local baseball team, once hitting three home runs for the Whittemore Pink Sox and striking out sixteen batters. "Albert Eisele tried to imitate Babe Ruth, the heavy-hitting New Yorker, and pounded out three home runs during the game," the Whittemore paper reported in 1922.[1] And he was considered a good wrestler as well. He also directed the church choir and composed an "Agnus Dei" that the choir sang for many years, ac-

1

Albert played trombone and bass violin for a hometown dance band.

cording to a 1989 centennial history of St. Michael's.[2] He played a variety of musical instruments, including the trombone in a band that performed at a local dance pavilion—one of the photos from that period shows him holding a trombone, surrounded by a bass violin, two violins, a clarinet, and a mandolin. He was also an expert pool player who earned money by winning bets on games.

"Our Iowa farm home had a large attic, and we bought an old pool table and installed it," he recalled. "We cut a hole in the chimney and installed a heating stove, and while this stole some of the draft away from the kitchen stove, it never stole enough to prevent mother from making us three square meals a day, even though we put in most of our winter hours playing pool." He became so proficient, he wrote, that "having mastered the game of pool, we graduated to billiards." But he found it required different skills and gave it up because "a farm boy couldn't haul twenty loads of long-straw manure during the day and expect to play billiards in the evening," he later wrote. "How could we play billiards when we had to push 300-pound shoats up a chute into a triple-box wagon? How could we play billiards when we ate twelve to sixteen pancakes every morning? It couldn't be done."

He reminisced about his childhood as he recalled his father returning from visiting relatives in Illinois in 1900

Albert with a team of horses while planting corn.

when he was just three. "Of my childhood recollections, the earliest carry me back to my native state in Illinois. And of these precious first memories, one has to do with the return of my father from a home-seeking trip to Iowa. Vividly I recall his entrance of the kitchen, clad in his Sunday best, his face beaming, while in one hand he bore a small basket of plums" brought from his brother-in-law's farm in Iowa. He saw his father's action as proof that "there exists in every human heart a mysterious inner urge which will not permit a traveler to set homeward from a strange land without carrying with him grapes, pomegranates, and figs. When, after moving to Iowa [in 1902], my father visited Illinois for the first time, he brought with him at his return five or six ears of seed corn. After another visit, he brought a sackful of peaches. His third visit yielded a bag of hickory nuts." He attributed "this odd action" to "a desire in the traveler to furnish to the folk back home ocular proof of his visit to a strange land."

And in a 1927 article he wrote for a Dubuque Catholic newspaper, he recalled old men playing cards in the corner of a Whittemore store while "a miscellaneous assortment of spectators, commentators, advisors and critics" looked on. "All in all, it is quite a social corner: one to which I myself occasionally repair, especially in the wintertime when I want to warm up after a cold trip into town on the corn wagon." Although he said he had never used tobacco in any of its forms and never would, he admitted that it was "a tremendous factor for creating and strengthening friendships among men."

He helped his father farm their half-section, which in those days relied on horse power, the real kind. "We usually had ten or twelve horses on the place," he recalled. "In such a bunch there was always apt to be a balker. We had one horse named Jack, which father bought at a sale at a bargain price. 'He's a good buy,' he said. But that was before he hitched the horse to a load of oats. The horse gave one pull, then quit. He was a balker." A second balky horse his father had to contend with was named Billy. "It wasn't the right name. The horse should have had the fancy Derby name of 'Come Now.' We went to town one day with father to get a load of tile. We brought the tile home and drove out into the field, but there Billy stopped as soon as the wagon got on plowed ground. 'Come now! Come now!' father urged. But Billy refused to come, either now or later."

He also reminisced about a grasshopper plague he experienced as a boy. "Father had a sixty-acre field of oats, one side bordering on pasture," he wrote. "Grasshoppers are always more numerous in pastures, and they came into the oats and started to chew off heads. Father got the binder out, and began cutting, from early morning over noon and until late at night.

Every time he came along that pasture side we could see the clouds of grasshoppers flying inward in front of the binder. By the time the binder came around again, the hoppers had finished the new swath and were ready for the next one. In this manner, the binder chased the grasshoppers to the center of the field, while most of the kernels lay on the ground."

His later fiction was often based on youthful experiences, but once, the only time I know of, he used an actual real life account of an experience that was both frightening and hilarious to illustrate the anti-Catholicism he and his family sometimes encountered. In an unpublished story called "The Holy Explosions," he told how he and his cousin Eddie Kerchner, a classmate in parochial school, would stay at each other's home. "Eddie lived east of town and I west, and about twice a year, he'd come home with me from school and stay overnight, a social gesture which I in due time always returned. It was always pleasant to stay at my Uncle Jerome's, and I'm sure that Eddie equally enjoyed staying at our house," he recalled.

Albert with one of his prize hogs.

5

One October night as he arrived at Eddie's house, an itinerant Syrian pedlar appeared and asked for a night's lodging. His Uncle Jerome welcomed him and told the pedlar he admired his courage and stamina while carrying a pack must have weighed a hundred and fifty pounds. After joining them for supper, the pedlar went into an adjoining room, took out a prayer rug "and unashamedly performed his evening devotions." After rejoining the family in the living room, "Uncle Jerome informed him that he and his family were Catholic. At the word 'Catholic,' the pedlar visibly started, as though some one had jabbed him with a pin. Fear gleamed from his eyes and Uncle Jerome didn't know what he found out later, that the pedlar has spent the previous night with the Wilbur Greens, who were notorious Catholic haters. He was certain that they had told the pedlar terrifying tales about Catholics. But he gradually calmed down and Uncle Jerome called his family together for its own evening devotions.

"Now my Uncle Jerome had come from Germany, from Westphalia, where on great feast days of the Church, instead of the traditional bells at the solemn climax of the Mass, cannons were fired outdoors. Such emphatic gestures had always deeply impressed Uncle Jerome and he had contrived to likewise enhance the family devotions by the use of explosives. It was always at the "Lamb of God" ejaculations near the end of devotions that one of the boys, usually Eddie, stationed in the pantry, would fire a shotgun out of a window into the sky. Three times Uncle Jerome would intone 'Lamb of God," then three times Eddie would fire his shotgun.

"Now the devotions that evening were held in the sitting room, the pedlar having moved into the kitchen, where, looking uneasy and frightened and no doubt wonder if he'd ever escape alive from this den of monsters, he kept sharp watch out of the corner of an eye. Eddie, in the meantime, was out of sight in the pantry. All went well until Uncle Jerome intoned the first 'Lamb of God' and Eddie fired, the blast rocking the house. The pedlar leaped straight out of his chair. 'Lamb of God,' said Uncle Jerome again, and once more, the shotgun thundered. The pedlar by this time was out of the house, taking part of the screen door with him. Outside it was pitch dark, and the pedlar ran into a wheelbarrow by the barn. The commotion caused Eddie to unconsciously lower his gun. 'Lamb of God,' said Uncle Jerome for the third time. The shotgun spoke, followed by a cry of terror in the night, and then the sound of a board fence splintering. The next morning we found a hole in the fence, with the surrounding boards peppered with birdshot. The pedlar never did come back for his pack, and Uncle Jerome felt badly about that. The pack was finally stored in the attic of his house, and is probably there yet."

In 1944, my father praised another cousin named George Elbert and his son after they captured two German prisoners of war who escaped from a POW camp near Whittemore. "The Elbert parent stock all came from Germany. All of the older generation can speak German, and taken as a whole, there are no better patriots or more loyal citizens anywhere. In this country, we have Polish-Americans, Swedish-Americans. Irish-Americans, and many other hyphenated groups. There are no German-Americans, and the upshot of this, in the long run, will be that America's best citizens will be those of German descent. Let all Americans of German descent strictly avoid and forget the hyphen, and they will in time provide an example to Americans of other descents."

On another occasion, he explained why he never served in the First World War. "We did not register until 1918 [when he was twenty-two] when our number came up in that class to be inducted, curiously enough, on November 11, 1918. Of course, we never went. Nevertheless, there were people who thought we should have enlisted. They said, 'Just wait till the boys come home—they'll fix you!' We shivered in our shoes. When the boys come home they would take us for a cleaning. They would blacken our eyes and punch our nose. The first boy to come home was one we had played ball with on the home team. We avoided him as long as we could but one day ran into him on the street. He shook our hand and greeted us warmly. We couldn't understand it. The other boys came home from Europe. How many of them punched us in the nose? Not one. How many of them jeered at us as a slacker? Not one. . . . Our boys, when they do come home, will have more sense than all of us noisy stay-at-homes put together."

My father originally wanted to be a cartoonist or poet, but decided he wanted to be a writer instead. Although I did not find any of his cartoons—or correspondence—in the voluminous papers he left, I remember the chalk talks he gave to amuse us or to illustrate points he made at local Farm Bureau or neighborhood meetings. Actually, there was little among his papers about his recollections of his early life, except for photographs of him on the farm with his parents and siblings, and newspaper clippings about his baseball games. Although he was close to his older sister and three younger sisters and brother, he seldom wrote about them or his mother.

But many of his short stories and columns were based on the experiences he had as a boy. In one "Post Chaise" column about the development of power on the farm over the past century, he told how his father drilled a well on their farm with the power furnished by teams of horses "going around and around. In the middle and directly over the horses was a platform on which sat a man with a long whip. . . . We also saw horse power furnish the energy needed to shell corn, saw wood and bale hay. We cannot remember seeing any threshing done by horse power, although considerable of it was still being done in that day. The first threshing that we remember was that done by steam engine. The steam engine was really the beginning of the machine age on the farms of America."

My father lived at home while helping run the family farm until marrying my mother when he was thirty-one. But his youthful experiences in an Iowa farm community provided the grist for what would prove to be a prolific literary mill.

Notes

[1] In 1994, the newspaper published a photo of him and his teammates when *Field of Dreams*, the movie about an Iowa baseball team in the 1920s, was released, saying that they "didn't need a Hollywood movie to show them a baseball field, and they didn't have to float like spirits out of a cornfield because all their lives they planted, plowed and picked corn."

[2] It contained profiles of many of the families who came to Whittemore from the same area of Illinois as other Germans, including those who married my grandmother's sisters, such as the Elberts, Fandels, and Kerchers, as well as the families of my father's siblings.

Chapter Two

Daughter of the South

MY MOTHER'S PARENTS WERE Irish and Swiss immigrants who came to America in search of a better life, unburdened by the heavy hand of history. Her father, Peter Frawley, left County Clare, Ireland, in 1883 at the age of twenty with a younger brother, escaping from a country still struggling to recover from the devastating effect of the Great Potato Famine. A saw filer by trade, he found work harvesting timber for railroad ties for the Great Northern Railway in Wisconsin. Her mother, Rose, was born in Altdorf, Switzerland, in 1875 in a house on the town square overlooking a statue of the fourteenth century Swiss patriot William Tell. In 1884, she came to America with her mother to join her father, Alois Huser, who had immigrated to Staten Island, New York, two years earlier and was working on a dairy farm. In 1886, they moved to central Wisconsin, where he homesteaded in Wood Country near the village of Altdorf, founded by Swiss immigrants.[1] She was still living at home and teaching in a country school ten years later when she met my grandfather at a church social.

They were married in 1896 before Peter Frawley's work took them to Mississippi and then to the Low Country of South

Carolina, where my mother was born in 1897, the first of ten children. "I was born in Georgetown, some sixty miles up the Atlantic coast from Charleston," she wrote me in 1979 when I told her I was planning to visit Georgetown. "Papa and Mama had just moved there from Mississippi as Papa's saw filing work moved him around to the areas that were most productive for milling lumber. They were staying at a boarding house that faced the docks and waterfront of Winyah Bay, which was then a busy shipping cen-

Susan as reporter in Tennessee.

ter. I was born on the second floor of a boarding house or kind of hotel that was run by two middle-aged sisters from Ireland, Miss Nonnie and Miss Norah—I wonder if it is still standing? They catered to the sailors and sea captains of the vessels coming and going from there. Soon after I was born, we moved next door to an apartment over a Chinese laundry, and then we moved to a house in the residential section on St. James Street."

She had "an enchanted childhood," she recalled. "My father's mill at the Atlantic Coast Lumber Company was across Winyah Bay, and the employees had to take a rowboat to get there. Sometimes he would take me to the mill with him, and I roamed around at random. There were copperheads and white-mouthed moccasins lurking in the tall grasses but luckily, I never got bitten. Then Papa said I was getting to be too big a little girl to be hanging around a saw mill. He was the heart of charity and often brought an ailing sea captain to our home for Mama to feed him some of her chicken soup. We heard stories from all over the world. One of the sea captains gave us a barrel of oranges. While they lasted, we were the most popular family in Georgetown. Otherwise, oranges were a luxury item and only came in the Christmas stockings. It was my job to take Papa's white shirts to the Chinese laundry. I loved that job. I liked the way the laundry smelled. A strange oriental fragrance was there."

In 1940, she told readers of one of the columns she later wrote about living "on the enchanted shores of the Carolina coast. After breakfast, we children would race over the ledges of sandhills fronting our palmetto-log summer cottage, down to the beach itself. There we looked for the water-filled depressions along its length . . . where porpoises had frisked and wallowed the night before. How good it felt to flop down in those sun-warmed pools of shallow water! Always the roundest and smoothest of the pools we saved for the baby, who was left there twice a day to frolic in safety while the rest of the family enjoyed the surf. . . . We get the same thrill over the little tracks in the snow that we did when we used to tramp over hot sand." And because she lived across from the opera house, as a pre-schooler she'd sneak over and watch rehearsals when "the then-great singers, dancers, and actors came to our town up the coast from Charleston as they toured the eastern coast. Ever since I was a little girl, I've liked live theatre better than any other form of entertainment."

She recalled accompanying her father to a gambling casino aboard an excursion steamship in Charleston when she was a girl. "Papa was good about showing me everything and I was full of curiosity," she wrote. "When we went into the casino, I was intrigued with the gambling devices and wanted to operate one of them. I was too young to know nickels from dimes or what a game of chance really meant. So Papa gave me some coins and went over to the soda fountain to get out some Coca Colas, our favorite drink. I put some coins in the machine but nothing happened. Then suddenly, coins began falling out, a bell was ringing and the machine lit up in many colored lights. I was frightened. I was wearing a fancy apron over a dress, and I tried to gather up the coins as they spilled to the floor. Papa came over and began laughing, and I began crying. I told him I was sorry I had broken the machine. He said I had not broken it but that I had hit the jackpot. I didn't know what that meant. Some of the men patted me on the head and called me a lucky little girl. When we got home, Papa told Mama what had happened and she said, 'Peter, you shouldn't have let her gamble!'"

Her family worshipped at a small Catholic mission church across the street from Georgetown's historic Prince George Winyah Episcopal Church, and often visited its cemetery, where her younger brother and sister were buried. "Mama and Papa used to take us for walks, and we would go to their little graves and say a prayer and then beg to go through the Episcopal church," she wrote. "And we would spend our summers on Pawley's Island. We could go out our back door and gather a dishpan full of oysters at low tide. We had lobster pots and fish nets, and we lived on seafood."

Even though her father had no formal education, he insisted "that we children get a good education, and I still have a set of the Harvard Classics he bought for us. Next, he bought us a typewriter. I learned to use it with the hunt-and-peck system. Mostly, Papa told me stories about Ireland and related many of its historic facts and folklore. He was a poet at heart. While Mama thought I should be taught some practical things like learning to cook and help with housecleaning, Papa would laugh and tell her to forget the dishes and come for a boat ride. Occasionally, Papa was laid off until more lumber could be shipped in, so Mama would stir up some of her cinnamon rolls or coffee cake and sell it at the fire stations. We were never cold or hungry or poorly clad." She added, "Papa never drank or smoked or ran around with other women. He had his prejudices, though. He was Irish, Catholic and a Democrat, and I really think he believed that was the only true combination to get into heaven." But it was her Swiss-born mother, she said, "who gave me a great sense of citizenship. She was so proud of the right to vote that I never missed a chance to cast a ballot since I came of voting age."

In 1905, her father's job took the family, which now included five children, to Newport, Tennessee, in the scenic Smoky Mountains. They were the only Catholic family in Cocke County, and soon learned they were in the heart of the Bible Belt. Shortly after they arrived in Newport, the Ku Klux Klan burned a cross one night in their front yard. But it was an isolated incident, and they were soon made to feel welcome by their neighbors.[2] As Marjorie McMahan, whose family lived two doors away, wrote in the Newport newspaper in 1972, "These fine people were of the Catholic faith, and they were dedicated and devoted to their religious convictions. My mother regarded Mrs. Frawley highly and spoke of her often as a good woman and a wonderful neighbor. She had been born in Switzerland and her husband in Ireland. This foreign quality added a glamour that those of us who were native to East Tennessee did not possess. . . . I still recall the home-made bread and the cinnamon rolls Mrs. Frawley baked often. . . . The fragrance from the oven of her old fashioned stove swept the length and breadth of Jones Hill."[3]

Years later, in one of her "Countryside columns, she wrote that St. Patrick's Day and recent race riots reminded her of how poor immigrants like her father succeeded in America. "As a minority group—I am speaking of the time when my own father came from Ireland, a young man with a brother and two sisters to look after. They didn't have a penny in the world. Their luggage was stolen at customs, and how they survived, I don't know. But they did, and they didn't protest with sticks and stones, but got to work and became good citizens. I think of other minority groups: the Poles, the Italians, the Scandinavians, all of them persecuted in one way or another. But they lived through it and have become good citizens. . . . You've got to wonder what it is that makes a person in a minority group work his way up in spite of the odds against him. And what makes another one bitter and feeling that the world owes him a living."

While she was obviously referring to the rioting then occurring in black inner cities, my mother always praised black people in her writings, although she never used the word "black" for Negro, and never forgot the lessons she learned from the black women who helped raise her in South Carolina and Tennessee. "No writer to my knowledge has ever given the American Negro the praise that he or she deserves," she wrote. "I've dreamed of writing a book about those valiant Negro mammies and maid servants who nursed us, spank us when we got unruly, and helped make life easier for our families. All this despite the injustices that were sometimes inflicted upon them."[4]

And in another column, she recalled that her parents and Negro servants influenced her attitude toward the existence of ghosts. "My mother would not tolerate any talk about ghosts," she wrote. "I think if she had come on a ghost in the road, she would have just told it to go on back home. And I think it would have. But my father, having come from Ireland, was full of stories that would make your spine tingle. I suppose he embroidered some of them for us children, who would beg him to tell them to us on Sunday afternoon expeditions into the pine woods of South Carolina. [But] our Negro mammies were the best ghost story tellers. I think Negroes, especially the older ones, so fresh from Africa and its strange rituals, are clairvoyant. The Negro woman who worked for us in Tennessee when my mother died, told us some weird things just before her death, and sure enough, they came true. So you can't actually say that there are or that there are not ghosts."

In 1907, Father Emmanuel Callahan, a horseback-riding missionary priest from Knoxville who ministered to Catholics in more than thirty counties in East Tennessee, celebrated Mass in the Frawleys' living room. He used their home to publish the first Catholic newspaper in east Tennessee, and the Frawleys set the type and sewed its pages together. They later offered Father Callahan part of their property for the chapel built in 1913. "The Frawleys donated land for a small and lovely Catholic chapel to be erected," Marjorie McMahan wrote as she recalled visiting St. Agnes Chapel. "Even as children, we were allowed to walk the aisle and gaze in wonder at the figures lining the walls. I learned the meaning of a crucifix and the significance of a rosary back then. I also learned how beautiful and how rare is the atmosphere of reverence in the house of God." On one occasion, Mrs. Frawley spoke to students at the Newport grammar school about the Catholic faith, which some parents later objected to.

It was in Newport where my mother began her writing career by reporting about her high school for the local newspaper. "I always wanted to write but there were no opportunities for me to do so while I was growing up," she recalled.[5] "I began writing high school notes for my hometown paper, the *Newport Plain Talk*," when I was thirteen. Then I wrote local news, feature articles, and finally editorials while the editor scrounged around for ads. It was a great experience." She added, "I'm not bragging, but I still have the clippings and they're not too bad."

After graduating from Newport High School in 1915, she enrolled in the American Academy of Christian Democracy for Women, an experimental school of social service that had just opened in nearby Hot Springs, North Carolina. The Academy was started by Father Peter Dietz, an activist labor priest from Milwaukee who had relentlessly badgered his superiors for permission to open the school. She was the youngest of seven students enrolled in a fourteen-week course that used as one of its basic texts, "Rerum Novarum," the 1891 papal encyclical in which Leo XIII addressed the condition of the working classes. Father Dietz imposed a strict discipline on his students. "With the exception of Wednesday and Saturday afternoon, which were free, practically every minute of the day was scheduled, from the rising hour, which varied from five to six-thirty with seasons, to lights out at nine or ten at night," his biographer wrote. "Study, recreation and prayer had their place in the order of the day. Spiritual motivation was further supplied in conferences by Father Dietz and in posted exhortations which encouraged meditation, examination of conscience, and spiritual reading."[6]

After reading the 1981 biography of Father Dietz, she wrote to a priest who had loaned her a copy, "Father Dietz was a saint, I think. He changed the course of my life." The book said she "credits Father Dietz with discovering her ability to write and forcing her to do so, often against her will." As she told the author, "I had lived in a fairyland until I met Father Dietz. Life was one grand sweet song. He showed me for the first time how serious life is, and how necessary it is for each of us to be our brother's keeper. . . . He made me aware of the suffering and injustice men inflict upon each other. . . . He taught me the dignity of labor and the duty of an employer to his employees."

He also changed her reading habits. "My favorite books were romantic novels, mystery stories, and popular women's magazines. But Father Dietz soon took me under his wing and began deprogramming me. 'Stop reading such junk!' he said. 'Read something worthwhile, the classics and such,' he ordered. The first book he handed me was Cervantes' *Don Quixote*. I nearly fell over. But to please him I took the book and began reading it. In no time I was convinced that Father Dietz knew what he was talking about."

There was another person in Hot Springs who expanded my mother's universe at the time. She was Bessie Rumbaugh Safford, a wealthy philanthropist and daughter of a tobacco magnate who offered Father Dietz the use of her estate for his new school. Mrs. Safford, whose first husband was the son of

President Andrew Johnson, was a Catholic convert and met my mother while attending mass that the missionary priest, Father Callahan, celebrated at the chapel on the Frawleys' property. "She is the woman who befriended me so richly," my mother wrote to me in 1979. "I think Father Callahan got her interested in me. She lived in a beautiful house, known as Chateau Loretto, in Hot Springs, which was about twenty-five miles from Newport, and invited me for weekends when she had interesting guests. She entertained lavishly, celebrities from all over the world. I met Cardinal Gibbons of Baltimore and other bishops and church dignitaries there, General Pershing, Russian counts and countesses. She had fabulous jewels and antiques all over the house, and servants galore and everything was formal, I loved every minute of it. Mama wasn't happy about my visits there. She was afraid I'd get spoiled and unhappy with our middle class life, but I didn't."

One of my mother's many vivid memories of Mrs. Safford was accompanying her on a hike in the Smoky Mountains. "She rode horseback and carried a pistol, and all of a sudden she said, 'I smell a rattlesnake.' And sure enough, there was one sunning itself on a pile of rocks. She took a stick and killed it. She was one of the finest and most interesting women I ever knew. Then, when I went to Knoxville, I kind of lost track of her, although she came to my wedding."

After returning from Hot Springs, my mother enrolled in the Knoxville Commercial College and took night classes at the Knoxville College of Law. She later became one of the first women in Tennessee to receive a law degree, but decided against practicing law. "This was somewhat unusual in those days because women just sat around and waited to get married," she told the *Newport Plain Dealer* in 1971. "But I never had a desire to practice law." Instead, she worked as an office manager, stenographer, and bookkeeper in Sevierville and Knoxville, while continuing to write and report for her hometown newspaper. In 1920, she began contributing to the *Daily American Tribune*, a Catholic newspaper in Dubuque, Iowa. Like her experience in Hot Springs, it turned her life in a new direction.

Notes

[1] Her mother's great-uncle, Fr. Anicet Regli, was the abbot of a Swiss Capuchin abbey who performed a famous exorcism of a young nun in the presence of her community in 1874. I was called by my middle name, Alois, until taking my father's name after his death.

[2] She was less charitable about the Klan and Southern society in a column she wrote for the *Daily American Tribune* in 1921. "I hate religious intolerance and I dislike anything that tends to aggravate this deplorable condition, but it is a striking fact that there is more illiteracy, more disregard for law and order, more crimes committed right here in our own beloved Southland, than in any other section of our country."

[3] In 2005, the *Newport Plain Talk* published a special section on the town's history. According to Editor Duay O'Neill, Mrs. Frawley was praised for her willingness to go into the homes of the ill and nurse them during the worldwide flu epidemic of 1918. She helped care for a young girl who lived across the street from her, who died, and when a young Catholic couple lost their baby, she was the only person who knew the proper responses at the funeral rites. The baby was buried in the Frawley family plot in the Newport cemetery but without a marker.

[4] Her opposition to abortion would place her among today's "pro-lifers." In a 1980 "Countryside" column, she promised to share "if my editors let me," a letter she once wrote her mother. "It starts out, 'Dear Mama: Thank you for not aborting me.' I think of it every time I see or hear or do something exciting."

[5] But she remembered that as a little girl, she wrote her first stories in scrapbooks her mother made for her, and hid them behind a brick chimney beside her parents' bedroom, and "no one else in the whole world knew about that grand hiding place."

[6] *Peter E. Dietz, Labor Priest*, by Mary Harrita Fox, University of Notre Dame Press, 1981.

Chapter Three

"A.A.E." and "Just Susan"

M Y PARENTS BEGAN THEIR long-distance relationship in the early 1920s as a result of their writing. My mother was working as a bookkeeper and stenographer in Knoxville, Tennessee, while attending business college and law school at night, and my father was helping run the family farm in Iowa when they began contributing to the young people's page of the *Daily American Tribune*, a new national Catholic newspaper in Dubuque, Iowa (its name was later changed to the *Catholic Daily Tribune*). She wrote a column of personal commentary under the byline of "Just Susan" or "Susan Frawley," while his articles, mostly short stories but often personal commentary as well, were signed "A.A.E.," or "With A.A.E." or "Albert Eisele."

The first of more than a hundred of his short stories, columns, and poems appeared in the publication's November 29, 1920, issue. Billed as the "Special

Two correspondents for Catholic young people's newspaper.

by Albert Eisele" and titled "The Voice of Love," it was illustrated with a photograph of the handsome twenty-four-year-old author, his hair slicked back and wearing a tie with stiff collar. It told the story of Otto Wurzberger, a painfully shy forty-five-year-old farmhand who was afraid to tell the forty-something woman he was courting that he was in love with her and wanted to marry her. Finally working up his courage, he vowed he would "declare his love for Mathilda or die in the attempt." But again, he remained tongue-tied until he decided that "in that utter silence spoke the Voice of Love. The most natural thing in the world for Otto to do was to take Mathilda in his arms and tell her he loved her. He did it," and blurted out the words, but in German. *"Zwei wei Seelan und einer Gedanke, zwei Herzen und einer Schlag."* ("Two souls and one thought, two hearts and one beat.") The story concluded, "And so we leave them." It was one of the only times my father used the language of his parents in his stories.

His articles often appeared on the front page with his photograph. Many of his short stories were anything but short, often 5,000 words or more. Almost all depicted some aspect of life in the rural Midwest in the early twentieth century, from planting and harvesting grain, attending county fairs and celebratory wedding feasts, Turgenev-like descriptions of the landscape and weather, sumptuous meals prepared by farmers' wives for threshing crews, and the struggles of parish priests and farmers and merchants in their daily lives, which were common themes of all his writing. Indeed, he drew inspiration from his closeness to the soil, and he proclaimed he was proud to be a farmer "for as long as I live."

His columns were intensely personal, as the one in June 1921 that bore the headline, "The Promised Letter from

Eisele." Written on his twenty-fifth birthday, its dateline was his hometown of Whittemore. He acknowledged "the flattering headline the good editor gives this letter," but said he'd "give a whole lot just to happen upon an original idea, that I might expand lazily over it. An original idea, it has been said, comes to a mind about once in a lifetime. While I passed this month my quarter-century birthday, I have not yet come in contact with that allowable fire-new motion—though I sit at the mouse-hole of my imagination with some degree of feline patience and tension. I have a dim memory of some character of *Alice in Wonderland* being obliged to think of seven original things before breakfast, the severity of which obligations I have never appreciated fully before. It seems we are living at such a late year that everything worthwhile has long since been written of or discovered. . . . Even original sin is getting common."

He focused on subjects ranging from threshing to baseball to bachelor romances, often in the same issue or on the same page as my mother's columns. It was obviously how they first took notice of each other. In 1921, for example, he commented on one of my mother's columns about men snoring. "I certainly enjoy the writings of Susan of Tenn., such life and vivacity! And I am rarely given such a distinct shock when I found her saddling up on the genius husband the terrific phrase 'perpetual burglar alarm!'—in allusion to snoring. The most alarming effect of this characterization is that it makes yet more shy and unapproachable those delicate creatures whom a lot of us fellows would like to 'carry and wive.' So I must attack Susan's scarecrow and scatter his coarse 'innards' to the four winds."

Later, writing about his own scarecrows on May 25, 1925, he took note of a column by my mother in which she

TINY AMERICAN TRIBUNE

TWICE-A-WEEK SUPPLEMENT TO THE DAILY AMERICAN TRIBUNE

DUBUQUE, IOWA, JULY 28, 1925.

Flora Meets Another Friend of Y. P. Club

DAYTON UNCONCERNED ABOUT SCOPES TRIAL

WHAT'S ON YOUR MIND?

With A. A. E.

One of the Catholic young people's newspapers Susan and Albert wrote for.

had made a scarecrow. "Did Susan Frawley wish to hang some old clothes in a stick in her garden, she could do naught better than to hang up the old clothes of some Hindu fakir. Can anyone imagine Tennessee birds alighting on that?"

In 1921, when a reader asked what the second letter of his byline, "A.A.E." stood for, he held a contest to guess what it was. My mother offered several guesses, which prompted him to write, "Among others, I was pleased with Anthony, honored by Adam, touched by Aloyious, surprised by Adolphus, puzzled by Antonio, exalted by Abraham, flattered by Alexander and thunderstruck by Aesculapius." He then wrote that he had forgotten that a reader was limited to only one guess, adding, "Just Susan, your guess is correct—that is one of them. Now, if I were to act real, real mean, I'd simply tell you that you won, that your guess was correct. But that wouldn't satisfy your curiosity, so you'd better take another guess as to which one of that list of yours is the one. And by the way, Susan, (to be a little curious myself), didn't you get that list—beginning with Abel and ending with Augustine – from the back of Webster's? Now didn't you?"

My mother responded with an indignant column "Did you ever hear of such monumental nerve? First he asks me to guess his middle name and after I go to work and unearth my trusty Webster and turn to the list of names for 'men only.' After I eliminate all the names of heathen gods and Hebrew men of fame and boil the A's down to a couple of dozen or so, in order to find IT—he comes along and says only one guess to a reader! Well, I might have known better! Anyway, I'm going to say right now that it's Ambrose. So tell us, please, Mr. Albert Anonymous Eisele!" (He later told her and other readers that his middle name was Arnold.)

But he also praised her as a promising writer. In a letter to the editor that same year thanking him for removing a word limit on submissions, he wrote, "When Nic Gonner set aside a space in his paper for the young people, it was his hope, we are told, of perhaps bringing to light a Catholic writer or two. Thus far we have accomplished little in that direction—all the more deplorable when one realizes that in these States, the ranks of good Catholic writers are badly thin. Susan Frawley is, I believe, our greatest hope at thus this time." My mother sent him a note, "Albert, this is so sweet of you!"

My mother usually wrote in the same vein as my father, about her experiences as a young woman, family, and friends, the scenic Smoky Mountains of east Tennessee, and religious bias she encountered as a Catholic. In her first column, which appeared on March 17, 1920, and datelined Newport, she invited readers to describe their most embarrassing moment, and then told of hers. It was during a train ride that had been delayed by a wreck, and she had struck up a conversation with a fellow passenger. She was vexed because the delay prevented her from meeting a friend's friend from the University of Tennessee in Knoxville, whom she was anxious to meet. "They say he is such a nice boy and comes from such a splendid family etc. etc.," she said. When asked the boy's name, she said, "I think it is Henry Mason." To which her fellow passenger replied, "Well, I happen to be Henry Mason." "Needless to say," she wrote, "I was never so chagrined in my life."

In a 1921 column, she responded to "Margaret" of Quincy, Illinois, who was torn between accepting a marriage proposal and pursuing a career. "I'm twenty-three—but I've lived a great deal longer than twenty-three years," she wrote. "I've been in commercial work for several years—they shoved me out of school when I was still a 'flapper—and am well on my way toward my goal of my ambitions in the world of business. But this hasn't spoiled me for the better things of life. By this I simply mean the things that you fear might obliterate your career—beaus, bungalows and babies." She defended marriage as "the biggest sort of career, even as big as dancing or writing or painting," and asked, "Why do you want to be immune from matrimony? I don't believe you'll ever be because Cupid's a funny cuss, and he'll shoot you full of dope some day. So for goodness sake, take it back before he hears you."

She also strongly defended her Catholic faith, writing in another 1921 column about a respected physician she knew who disowned his son because he was marrying a Catholic. And she related the conversation she overheard when the physician told a colleague why he forbade the son to come home with his bride-to-be. "I suppose it was dreadfully wicked of me to listen," she wrote, but she heard him say that his son's decision to marry a Catholic had "shattered" his hopes and dreams. She concluded, "If you have ever lived in a town like ours, where Catholics and popery and nunneries are taboo subjects, where they think a crucifix is an article of Catholic jewelry, where they breed religious intolerance among their own sects—then you'll be able to appreciate the cause of Dr. Shelby's illness. But as the years pass on, the Shelbys may become reconciled, their disgrace may be forgotten—in view of the fact that the Chinese proverb says, 'It is not polite to talk about hanging men to those whose fathers have hung.'"

In another 1921 column, headlined "What Does an Old Maid Think About?" she declared that Mark Twain "knew a lot about boys but he didn't understand girls" because they "are such complicated affairs." She added, "Almost every girl would prefer to be a widow than an old maid . . . Probably because old maids remind us of so many things, like green parrots and black cats and shabby geraniums and serge skirts and teaching music and dying with pleurisy. . . . Widows conjure up a number of interesting experiences and becoming black lace veils and violet-scented handkerchiefs and soft sighs and pressed flowers and eternal hope." So she cautioned women torn between marriage and career to "pack up your career very carefully and put it away in the attic with all the discarded furniture and your first attempts to become an artist and your party dress that got too little and the cracked vases and torn books—sometime you will want to show them to your grandchildren—and maybe they will be wiser than you and they will smile sadly at your foolish attempts to wreck your own life. So don't regret that you chose the white bungalow and the sunsets—they will last forever."

My father often referred to and commented on my mother's columns, and he undoubtedly read her thoughts about old maids and marriage with interest. But the one that must have really caught his attention was one she wrote in March 1925 entitled "Aren't Men Queer? In it, she recounted her experience with two men she'd been seeing in Knoxville while working and attending a business college and a law

28

school at night. "I don't know how it all happened. It was so unexpected," she wrote. "Men are so brutally frank about some things. They do not realize how it hurts a woman to have unkind things said to her. Being men, how can they understand? But they do not have to be so unkind."

She explained that her friend Bob was "dreadfully old-fashioned" because he thought "a woman ought to stay at home and cook and that is foolish for her to want a career. He ought to know that sooner or later, every woman wants a career. It makes better wives and mothers out of them because they appreciate a home then. That's how it started. I was taking extra law lectures two nights a week, and he thought that was too much. I didn't say anything to him last winter when he took up the lectures on business administration. That was *three* nights a week. . . . Well, if my husband is going to be one of those narrow-minded gentlemen who will not let his wife even think for herself—I won't get married! I've seen *entirely* too much of men to ever want to marry one of them! It's hard enough to just be friends with them!" That led to an argument, and he walked out, forgetting to take his Chesterfield cigarettes, and was furious when he came back to get them, and she told him she'd thrown them in the fire. She cried herself to sleep after deciding that she "just *hated* men!"

But there was another man in her law classes she liked. "True, he did wear sideburns and a wristwatch, but otherwise he was perfectly normal . . . Mr. Harrison, who wanted me to call him by his first name, but I didn't, came up once or twice a week after supper, to talk over court procedure or real property with him—which are the most difficult parts of the law for me to grasp." But he quit coming when he learned that she was seeing Bob, who had called twice, but she said she was busy. Then she spotted Bob driving with a blonde woman at his side, which sent her into a tailspin. "It seemed to me that I lived in a trance for several days. Every time I went anywhere, I saw Bob and the blonde woman," and when he tried to introduce her, my mother "would adroitly turn the corner, or engage in spirited conversation with the nearest passerby. I know it was silly, but I couldn't get interested in my law lectures any more. Suddenly they seemed to grow dry and insipid. I am ashamed to say it, but even the *moonlight* wasn't silvery any more, and I couldn't look at the *stars* like I could when Bob was with me—now they were just *stars!*"

Then, one night she went for a walk near her house and was surprised to hear Bob's voice. "I was so happy—then I remembered the blonde woman. Oh, dear, I might be eavesdropping. What was *he* doing up there? . . . Then I called over to him. "Bob." I don't remember what he said, but he came over to me and he looked so *funny!* . . . He told me he thought he would come up into the moonlight and see if it wouldn't make him feel better, but it only made him feel worse. . . . I told him I was sorry he hadn't been feeling well and in the most *casual* manner, asked him what had been the matter, and he said I knew good and well what had been the matter. He said that 'those darned bob-haired aunts got his goat.' Then I realized the blonde-haired woman was his *aunt!* And he walked home with me and I knew *instinctively* that the war was over. And I was very *impersonal* but he told me *a lot of personal things*, and wonder of wonders, he said he would help me with court procedure and real property. . . . Aren't *men* queer? But I like them!"

That same summer, after receiving a letter from the editor of the *Newport Plain Talk*, saying its readers "missed the communications you used to send us" and asking if she could "find time to send us a few lines occasionally, she decided to cover the historic 1925 Scopes "monkey trial" in nearby Dayton, Tennessee. "All I was interested in was seeing Scopes and Darrow and Bryan, and I couldn't stay there too long," she recalled in a letter to my daughter Kitty in 1976. "Also, I was young and inexperienced and didn't know my way around too well, but I just stuck my neck out and went by train to Dayton."

Clarence Darrow and William Jennings Bryan of Nebraska were opposing attorneys in the trial of John Scopes, a public school teacher accused of teaching the Darwinian theory of evolution. Darrow, one of the most famous lawyers in America, was defending Scopes, while Bryan, the "Great Commoner" and three-time Democratic presidential nominee, was his chief prosecutor. "Darrow was a so-called atheist, but a friend of mine who was in Darrow's party when he beheld the majesty of the Smoky Mountains, said, 'There must be a God to have created such beauty.' I liked him from the start and think he was a great man." Although Scopes was found guilty, Bryan was humiliated by Darrow's relentless cross-examination, and died a few days later, a death some said was hastened by the rigors of the trial. "Bryan died right after the trial and his funeral train stopped in Knoxville right behind the office where I was working, and we had a good view of the train," she recalled. "I think the trial killed him."[1]

But she left little doubt how she felt about the theory of evolution or those who opposed teaching it in Tennessee schools. In an article for the *Daily American Tribune* headlined "Dayton Unconcerned about Scopes Trial," she wrote: "Maybe you will wonder what I saw at Dayton during the first days of the Scopes trial. It did not seem to make any difference to the inhabitants of the town as to what was happening in the court house. Their apparent nonchalance was the most surprising thing I noticed. As far as knowing what was happening, you keep up with it just as easily by reading the papers as if you were sitting in a reporter's seat in the front row. I am a Tennessean by adoption, but I regard the passage of the anti-evolution law as the most unconstitutional law that has ever been passed by an American state. The Bible. You would think that the lawmakers and the governor of Tennessee regard themselves as divinely appointed guardians of the Bible and its temporal and spiritual welfare. It is all very ridiculous to me. Tennessee has long been known as the state with a million laws.

"If evolution and the Biblical story of creation conflict, then this question is a fundamentally religious question. If this is true, no legislative body has a right to interfere or exercise its jurisdiction in matters pertaining to the church, or religion, if you please. If, on the other hand, this question of evolution does not conflict with the Bible, or if it is a scientific question, then it might properly come within the apparent scope the State's authority. And the vicious circle is complete. Tennessee claims that evolution does conflict with the Bible —then it allows one of its judges (a country judge at that) to rule it out as a testimony. The question might become too complicated—for as Darrow says stubbornly, 'What Bible?' One of the fifty-seven varieties certainly, but which one? So we will follow the case with the greatest of interest."

She concluded with a scathing appraisal of the people of Dayton, and her fellow citizens of Tennessee. "They are fundamentalists because they have not the courage to look beyond their own narrow horizons and see that the other fellow has the same protection under the laws of this country as they have.

That is what is the matter with Tennessee—it needs to have a little more tolerance and a lot more liberty. France ought to send over another lady with a torch and plant it right down here."

Not surprisingly, she grew to like her fellow correspondent from Iowa even though she had never met him and didn't know much about him. But they got to know each other better through their correspondence. He described their long-distance romance when he guest edited her "Penny Pencil" column after she was named the nation's outstanding rural journalist by *County Home Magazine* in 1936.

"It was along about in 1920 that Susan Frawley of Tennessee and this writer, then of Iowa, became contributors to a young people's literary department of the Dubuque paper," he recalled. "We both contributed regularly for a period of five or six years; then one day, this writer addressed a letter to Susan Frawley, asking whether she could provide us with some information on the leg-of-mutton. . . . Susan Frawley looked up some notes on the subject and passed them on to us. That was fine—except that she typed her notes on the back of our letter. And that made us furious. We wrote her again and said, 'Your writing betrays a poetic nature and a certain facility in writing, but unless you make your subject matter something more than froth, you may as well go back to dish-washing and save yourself future heartaches.' And that made *her* furious, and a fierce paper war resulted. This paper war finally settled, but alas, the fatal spark had been set. This was in 1926, and the two of us then wrote one, two, and often three letters daily till February 1927, when this writer, badly frightened, boarded a train at Algona, Iowa, on his way to visit a girl to whom he was practically engaged but who he had not even seen.

Susan's photo of Albert during visit to Tennessee in 1927.

"'He's crazy!' said our parents. 'He'll get murdered!' wailed an aunt. 'Tie him to a tree till he gets over it,' suggest a neighbor. But father carried us on over the humming rails, and when the Southland Flyer drew into Knoxville, Tennessee, one sunny day in February 1927, a sensitive and intellectual girl stood on the platform and watched the Chicago coach for the appearance of a 'tall, dark young man dressed in a dark suit and a light hat.' Now it happened that this writer wasn't the first one out of that Chicago coach; in fact, he was last—the conductor had to push us out. . . . All the other men preceded us; one was tall and dark, and dressed in a dark suit and light hat; he scowled terribly, had a livid scar running from his forehead to his collar, was greasy, and looked like a Chicago gangster. Just why Susan Frawley did not faint at sight of this fake Romeo we have never been able to understand. But she didn't, and we stumbled out on the platform at last, stumbled toward the girl whom we recognized as Susan Frawley, shook hands with her and then and there laid forever that demon Doubt who had hounded us for every mile of that unforgettable journey."

He went on to note that he stayed in Knoxville for one week, "too happy to be real we thought; one week in fairyland. For we had found the girl of our dreams, and here was romance of the sort that not even the movies can portray. We went to shows, climbed some of the peaks of the Appalachians, wandered about the town, or just sat on the lawn under the stars and talked. Then—overnight, it seemed—the week was up and it was time to return to Iowa. 'I won't go along to the depot,' said Susan 'I'm afraid I'd cry.'"

But they continued their torrid correspondence, and at some point, he proposed to her. She said yes, and he made a second trip to Tennessee, to marry her in Newport on June 29, 1928, with her sister and brother, Caroline and Peter Frawley, Jr., as attendants.[2] The wedding was "in a little chapel on a hill, rice thrown, happy faces, congratulations— and, subsequently, an appalling drop in Uncle Sam's postal revenues," my father recalled. She wore cream chiffon dress and matching hat and carried a bouquet of roses, lilies, and larkspur as her parents and family and friends, including Bessie Rumbaugh Safford, the widow of the son of President Andrew Johnson, looked on. "Gone was the doubt, which had assailed us on the previous trip," my father wrote. "This time, our spirits were light and carefree—in fact, had the time been later in the year, we would have saved train fare by flying south with birds!"

Notes

[1] Ironically, Scopes, whose conviction was later overturned by the Tennessee Supreme Court, died on May 19, 1971, two days after she recalled covering his trial in an interview with her hometown newspaper, the *Newport Plain Talk*.

[2] It would be the last time she saw her father, who died a year later.

Albert and Susan pose for wedding photo with sister Caroline Frawley and brother Peter Frawley in 1928.

Chapter Four

Pilot Grove, Post Chaise, & Penny Pencil

MY PARENTS BEGAN their married life in 1928 on a 160-acre farm in Pilot Grove township in Faribault County, Minnesota. His father had bought the land in 1922 for $29,500 as an investment. Located in the midst of the Corn Belt midway between the county seat of Blue Earth and the town of Elmore on the Minnesota-Iowa border, it was a typical Midwestern small farm, with corn, oats, and soybeans the main crops, and populated by milk cows, pigs, and chickens. However, the Depression soon hit and even though his father had given them the farm—and the remaining mortgage—they were unable to make payments, and lost half the farm in 1930. But they worked hard and eventually paid off the mortgage. Their first children, twin boys Joseph and Francis were born in 1929, although the latter was stillborn. A daughter, Alberta, was born in 1930 and died on Christmas, 1932, a day after Arnold was born. A fifth child, Vincent, was born in 1934 but only lived a few months, and I was born in 1936, the last of their children.

Susan and Albert and their three boys on the farm in 1936.

After their marriage, my mother stopped writing for the *Daily American Tribune*, a Catholic newspaper in Dubuque, Iowa, which she and my father had contributed to since 1920, and plunged into her new role as a wife and mother. She had thought of the farm as a dull, uninteresting place where people stagnated intellectually and spiritually, but found it the best place in the world in which to live, to raise a family and grow in mind and spirit. She was happy to be a farmer's wife while raising a family and feeding the chickens, a life that "I loved and would have been satisfied doing" forever if not for a tragic event that led her to resume her writing.

The catalyst was the death of two-year-old Alberta on Christmas, 1932, one day after she gave birth to a son, Arnold, in the Blue Earth hospital. The little girl, who had been taken to a hospital in Mankato, died after contacting scarlet fever from a hired hand. "What really motivated me into starting this kind of writing was the death of our little girl, Alberta," she recalled. "Death seems to play an important part in our life. Albert and I were both so crushed by the suddenness and almost cruel blow that struck at us then, that we felt that nothing ever again could hurt us so much. And I felt that my sanity and perhaps faith were being weakened, and it frightened me. I plunged into the housework and the care of the

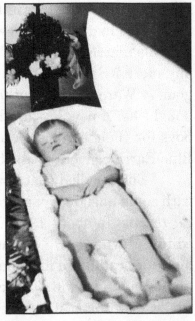

Alberta in her casket. She died on Christmas 1932 of scarlet fever at two.

new little son who came to us that Christmas Eve and who took in a good measure the place of the little girl who died that Christmas morning. But it wasn't enough.

"I think Albert saw plainer than I did, that I needed to go back to my writing, which I had almost given up when I married. I was happy just being a wife and a mother and writing seemed at that time to be unnecessary. I did a little, just enough to keep in practice. But Albert kept fussing at me. Being a wife and mother, he said, should make me a better writer. I should forget the rainbows and butterflies and the ephemeral things I had always written about, and write about the realities. The things about me, the life I was living, all the significant and beautiful aspects of marriage and a home. . . . Finally, he said, 'I think you are written out!' That did it. I'd show the man that I wasn't written out."

She had sold the new Royal typewriter she had before she was married after she "decided it had no place in my life any more." So she bought a rebuilt Underwood from Montgomery Ward, and used it for twenty years until her husband bought her a new Royal. The old typewriter was used by the boys for their homework and eventually given to nuns at a Blue Earth convent. "God bless that typewriter!" she wrote.

She recalled that "our formal column writing started with some unsigned paragraphs I wrote for the [weekly] *Blue Earth Post* in about 1932. I took a column or two up to the editor, Maynard "Pi" Johnson, and asked him if he thought his paper could use material of this kind. Mr. Johnson didn't know me and I didn't know him, but his promise that he would look the stuff over encouraged me more than he will even know. Albert and I had done this episodic, paragraphic form of writing for the *Daily American Tribune* in Dubuque,

Iowa, and had developed it into a unique kind of writing, which we had faith in, but did not know exactly how to present it to a public."

Johnson agreed to publish her work under the heading, "It Appears to Me," without a byline. "It must have clicked to a certain degree, and there was much talk around town as to who was writing it. Some friends accused me of writing it, and I was honestly afraid to admit that they guessed right. I remember the first paragraph in the first such column, which appeared in the *Blue Earth Post* had to do with the postage stamp. Then Albert began to take a great interest in it, and he was writing paragraphs 'just to help me out.' And the next thing I knew he was crowding me out entirely. About this time, we were getting reprints from other papers who had picked up our stuff, and I thought we might as well reveal our identity. I remember how thrilled we were over our first reprints! And how much we appreciated our hometown paper was giving us for our literary expression.

"About this time, too, the [daily] *Fairmont Sentinel* began quoting from our stuff. The editor, Major [Arthur] Nelson, was very understanding and appreciative of us, and I was emboldened to ask him if I could write a column for his paper. I reminded him as diplomatically as I could that it lacked a woman's touch, and I said maybe I could supply it. So the "With a Penny Pencil" column was born. Albert thought up the name. It started in May 1933. And Albert took over the column in the Blue Earth paper forthwith. Immediately it became a man's column. He changed the name to 'The Post Chaise.' And he let me understand that it was his column alone, he didn't need any meddling from me. But that was fine with me as I had my hands full with my new venture."

Later, in 1940, they began jointly writing a farm and home column for the Blue Earth paper called "Countryside," which was syndicated and appeared in some thirty Midwestern newspapers. Occasionally, the Blue Earth paper printed them side-by-side.

My mother once described her husband's writing philosophy by quoting from his first "Post Chaise" column: "Some day, a farmer will write the great American farm novel. Milking and cleaning out the barn and husking corn and shoveling paths though snowdrifts will not be menial peasantry to him—they will be life itself. When that man is born who can stay on the farm, love it and fight out his battles on the confines of his own land, see a beauty in it, who can feel his mind and soul and body responding and enlarging to the influences surrounding him—and who can then sit down after a hard day's work and write a little bit of himself on a little scrap of paper—then and only then is the great American farm novel going to be written. It will come not out of sophistication, but out of simplicity itself. It will be a story of grim tragedy and bitterness and disappointment, of course, but it will not be hopeless tragedy and bitterness and disappointment; rather it will be the epic of a soil triumphant, a beauty and mellowness and love that will reveal and portray the infinite bounty and goodness of God Himself."

My mother said the column "gave Albert the sense of editorial expression he needed. From his own profound mind, a closed book to me, one that I never did succeed in opening, and which no man or woman has any right to try to open because it is sacred and too integral, came his column writing. He did an enormous amount of reading. Slowly and deliberately, making notes as he went along. History, particularly of the American and European wars, the classics, especially Shakespeare, Cervantes, Dante, Carlyle, the essayists he devoured hungrily, short stories he searched out from every source, poetry too. Newspapers and magazines, preferably the editorial pages and the more intellectual types he studied carefully. He never catered to any cause or tried to slant his column writing to please any particular group. What he wrote he wrote because it was what he thought or felt, and he wanted to present his findings honestly and fairly as he saw the issue. He had few dislikes or hates. I think Franklin Roosevelt and Winston Churchill riled him up the most.[1] He considered them two of the world's worst rascals. He hated war in all forms and felt that the butchery of innocent young men called for the vengeance of heaven.

"I don't know where he got his political views. We differed some on them. But he had a keen sense of right and wrong and could analyze a political or military situation and quickly get at the basic issues. Many of his readers differed with him on his political views, even took exception to some of the things he said, but all of them read him and respected him nevertheless. Often someone wrote him to tell him they had been offended or that he had pointed a finger at them, it would happen that he had meant no offense or had wanted to talk in a general or impersonal manner about a certain subject. Most of this came from people who wanted to air a gripe or pet peeve. Once in a while, he got an anonymous letter or one from a crackpot. But considering the type of writing he did in his 'Post Chaise' column, he was remarkably free from this form of attack."

Mother said his readers were a "diverse group" ranging from students who asked him for advice and to critique their own writings, to professors and editors and "clergymen of all faiths with whom he carried on lengthy correspondence and from whom he derived much inspiration and encouragement." But he was also "read and appreciated by the ordinary man on the street and on the farm. If I may call this the most numerous and important of all men on earth, ordinary. And indeed, Albert and I have found in our writing that the unpretentious man or woman, who goes about quietly and may have little to say, has a wonderful mind and soul hidden under a very, shall we say, commonplace exterior." She described his sense of humor as "deep and sometimes bordered on the ribald. He often said that the use of humor was a very tricky literary medium. You have to use it skillfully if you use it at all. And he found himself often times bewildered by it."

Finally, she wrote that, as he grew older, he "slanted his writing to this group of readers, It was the smart thing to do. After all, they are the folks who buy the papers and read them. They are the folks who live and work and die with little or no fanfare, and they are the folks who wrote him or came to him and told him they liked his stuff because that was what they did and felt. 'Only you can write about it and we can't.' Maybe they could have, too, but just would rather do other things and let someone else do the writing. But be that as it may, Albert had a tremendous following, and he tried to give them his very best. That was why his 'Post Chaise' was his life."

My father, who continued to write for the Dubuque newspaper, now called *The Catholic Daily Tribune*, sometimes felt it necessary to defend himself and his literary style. In a March 3, 1931, column after a fellow columnist found two of his stories lacking in "plot" and "dramatic incident," he wrote, "I never aim at plot. If ever there is plot in one of my stories, then it has gotten there [unintentionally]. . . . I aim first of all to make my stories true to life. And no one had ever said that they are not that, though they have been criticized from all other angles. Plot in life seems to me always accidental; why should it be used in stories? Plot has no place in realistic writing." After another of his stories was called "aimless and vague," he responded, "I can only say that in each story that I write, I have an aim: to evoke either the spirit of tragedy, or the spirit of happiness. It is mostly tragedy to which I devote myself, because this spirit is nearer to the surface, is far more common; and because, I suppose, I have seen so much of it in the last ten or fifteen years here in the Middle West. To capture the spirit of tragedy is comparatively easy; to capture the spirit of happiness is exceedingly difficult. . . . And always, at all times and above all when I write, I seek to catch and mirror the beauty and significance of life."

He added, "I have chosen my medium, and am satisfied with it. It may get me nowhere as far as recognition is concerned, but that is of small moment here. I write from a desire to create and create artistically." At the same time, he went out of his way to "thank everyone who has ever encouraged me in any way . . . and wish to assure them that their good wishes have not gone unappreciated. That it is not my practice to publicly acknowledge such notices is due to two reasons: first, a lack of time, and second, the fact that such a procedure could bring into my conduct a great deal more pontificality than there is at present. And goodness knows, there is enough now."

He explained his research methods: "First of all, I keep a file of notes under such headings as AUNTS AND UNCLES, BASE-BALL, COURTSHIP, DROUGHT, FIELD AND STREAM, etc. I also keep notes classified as to the twelve months of the year, also the four seasons. When I get the idea for a story, I first set the time or year and lay the scene, then go through my notes selecting material accordingly. If my story has a harvest setting, then I consult the notes on 'HARVEST,' also under 'JULY,' which is the month of harvest. For the characters involved, I do research under those headings concerned with characters, as for example, 'CHARACTER TOUCHES,' 'MANNERISMS OF SPEECH AND DRESS,' 'QUAINT EXPRESSIONS,' etc. Usually I make a liberal selection of possible items to be used, but of course only a percentage of these are used. The great pitfall of such a method is that one will clutter up the story with detail. Just what detail to use and what to leave out is sometimes quite a problem.

He added, "It takes me about two weeks to complete a story, a story that runs usually between two and three thousand words. I have always believed in keeping a short story really short. This is a highly competitive age, with the radio and the movies vying with the writer, and I think the really short story has a better chance of being read, and also being remembered for more than a few days. I find the two- to three-thousand-word range ideal for the short story. Perhaps I have been prejudiced by the five- to ten-thousand stories that one finds so often in the household magazines.

"I think the thing for any writer to do is find his best medium and stick to it. I started out by writing poetry, wrote a hundred sonnets but couldn't publish any, so finally wrote in the simpler forms when I began publishing poems in *Spirit*. It was John Gilland Brunini, the editor of *Spirit*, who published my first poem and who also encouraged me in my prose writing. After getting into the swing of short story writing, I neglected my poetry, but have always wanted to return to it. I have also written a novel, but it has been roundly rejected and remains unpublished. Publishers have found it too slow-moving and too lacking in dramatic punch. I still think it to be a fairly good piece of writing, certainly as good as dozens of novels that are published each year and forgotten. I do think, however, that my forte lies in the shorter stuff."

My parents devoted most of their energies to operating their eighty-acre farm, while somehow finding time to write and raise a family. "A lot of work on the farm these days," my father recalled in one of his "Post Chaise" columns. "Plowing to be finished, chicken houses to be cleaned and repaired, corn to be snapped for the hogs, silos to be filled, gardens to be gathered in and plowed, a short string of tile to be put in (maybe), potatoes to be dug and stored and milkweed pods to be picked."

In a 1944 "Post Chaise' column, he wrote that his farming activities were little different from the thirties. "Our pig crop is in and is rather light. Last year we kept twelve sows for spring farrowing and raised ninety hogs. This year we kept ten sows and have less than fifty pigs. To begin with, two of the sows were barren and that left us only eight. Some had litters of three and four. One sow had a litter of eight, but she was like the elephant who saw a nest of hen's eggs uncovered and said, 'Look at those poor eggs getting cold! I'll sit on them myself.' Of course, there were no eggs left, and also no little pigs left after the sow had reposed herself directly upon them. Yes, we are going to cut down our hog production this year, but we didn't plan it that way." He added, "Soon now, we will have our baby chicks. We ordered these last winter—250 females at almost $70. That looks like an outrageously high price now. But we are not going to cancel the order. . . . We'd rather take a licking . . . than repudiate our signature. We preach intellectual honesty in this column, then we'd better practice it to the best of our ability." Mother also recalled that my father, who rarely drank any alcohol except beer, made grape wine and give it to friends. "Needless to say, he was a very popular man."

My parents were also active participants in church activities at Blue Earth's SS. Peter and Paul's Catholic Church, and in the local Farm Bureau and other civic groups. But the death of Vincent affected my mother deeply, especially after losing her two-year-old daughter two years earlier. As she recalled in a letter to me many years later, he "was a beautiful baby with lots of black hair . . . but he didn't grow like he should and we had difficulty with feeding him. But he seemed to get that straightened out and the doctor said we were over the hump. Then suddenly he got terribly sick. The George Carrs [neighbors] drove us to Rochester. It was a cold, icy night, and I was beside myself with grief and just about to lose my faith in God. One of the old nuns grabbed the baby and said, 'He's no good.' She must have known. . . . He had pneumonia and lived ten days and suffered terribly. They didn't want me to stay in the room with him as he was quarantined, but I did.

"The night he died, I asked them to get a priest, and they said he didn't need a priest, but I said he did. The chaplain lived nearby . . . He was an old French priest, and he was just wonderful, God bless him. He talked to me and made me feel better. He told me about the experiences he had in France with the men going to their execution, and I felt very near to God with him there. Soon after he left, Vincent died. I called an aide and told her and the sisters came streaming in, holy water and all. One of the younger nuns cried and knelt by Vincent a long time. . . . I forgot to tell you but just before Vincent died, [the]experience left me a different woman, and maybe Vincent had to suffer for me. Since then I have grown hardened and maybe I needed to. I don't think anything could shake my faith in God anymore. . . . Then you came along and brought a new joy into our lives. Albert wanted more children. He loved children."

But they both managed to make time for writing. My father did most of his writing early in the morning, between 4:00 and 5:00 a.m., by pencil on whatever paper was handy and then on an old Oliver typewriter in his book-lined study in the living room. He pounded out his weekly "Post Chaise" column, filled with homely philosophy and pithy comments on farming, politics, and current events, and even a novel, although it never got published.[2] Unlike my mother, he wrote slowly and painstakingly, making good use of the detailed files he kept of ideas that came to him as he worked in the fields or did farm chores. At first, he concentrated on poetry. His first poem was published by *Spirit Magazine* in July 1935. It was called "Harvest Moment," a four-stanza work of four lines each that described driving a horse-drawn binder to harvest "yellow grain that kinks (It's too ripe to stand)," while controlling "horses wet with sweat that wait my guiding hand." He wrote many other poems, including one obviously about my brother Arnold in 1934. It was called "Lines Addressed to a Two-Year-Old":

> Why bless you child, where did you find
> That wee, red pocket comb?
> You wish me now to be so kind
> Your tousled hair to plume?
>
> All right, hold still my little man,
> Let's make the part just so;
> We'll make of you a Don Juan
> Who may a-wooing go.
> One curl to this side, one to that,

And pat them down like this;
Each girl's heart will go pit-a-pat,
Each girl will want a kiss.

Ah, there! Your hair now seems to be
A bit of Irish lace—
Your hair is combed most beautifully,
But gosh! That dirty face!

But rather than poetry, my father turned more and more to short stories, which were soon to become his passion and his road to literary acclaim. But in June 1936, the literary spotlight turned first on my mother, thanks to her "Penny Pencil" column in the *Fairmont Sentinel*.

Notes

[1]Although he had "always been a Democrat, and always voted that ticket," he wrote in an October 31, 1944, "Post Chaise" column that he would not support Roosevelt's bid for a third term. "A third term would break down tradition, and if we break down one tradition, why not more? We are just pro-American enough to believe that traditions are sacred enough to be protected."

[2]Ironically, in light of his death from cancer in 1951, the novel's protagonist was a farmer who died of cancer.

Chapter Five

From Blue Earth to Broadway

I N THE SUMMER OF 1936, Arthur M. Nelson, publisher of the *Fairmont Sentinel*, submitted five of my mother's "Penny Pencil" columns to *The Country Home Magazine* in New York for consideration as the nation's outstanding rural columnist. She had only begun writing the column three years earlier after promising Nelson she would supply "a woman's touch" to his newspaper, and he submitted a half-dozen without telling her. Calling her a "talented writer worthy of a much larger audience than she has through our columns," Nelson declared, "in sixty-five years of publication, she is easily the most outstanding writer the *Sentinel* has had." He noted that she was a thirty-nine-year old farmer's wife who "does all her own housework, looks after several young children, and assists with the farm work in garden and poultry yard."

On June 26, the magazine's editor, Wheeler McMillan, informed Nelson that my mother had been awarded first prize for one of her columns about the threshing season, which had appeared in the Fairmont newspaper exactly one year earlier. The award included a $200 check and a trip to New York and

Mayor Yearns to Be Columnist

New York Mayor Fiorello LaGuardia presents Susan with six-foot replica of title of her prize-winning column, "With a Penny Pencil," 1936.

Washington. After excitingly informing Mother that she had won, Nelson drove the twenty-five miles to my parents' farm on June 28 to get a photo for the magazine. But she was about to give birth to the last of her six children, Albert Alois, and the photo shoot had to be delayed. "I was stunned," she said after learning of the award, "but the stork wasn't . . . he brought us an eight-pound son." When McMillan wrote a few days later, he congratulated her for "an additional reason for happiness in the birth of a son," and asked her to bring him along with her to New York in August for a public announcement. He also offered to pay for a "competent trained" nurse to accompany them. Nelson assured McMillan she would be able to make the trip as "she is in abundant health and wrote her usual 'Penny Pencil' column four days" after giving birth. He added, "The name is pronounced 'I-zel-E.' The accent is on the first syllable."

She traveled to New York and Washington in August, accompanied by her infant son and his nurse, Mrs. William Hynes, a neighbor and friend. It turned out to be an incredible experience, not only for the family archives, but for the history books as well. Her celebrity status is chronicled in the dozens of yellowed newspaper clippings and letters contained in a large scrapbook that she gave me shortly before her death in 1984. And even though I don't remember any of it since I was only seven weeks old, it's fair to say that my mother took New York City by storm.

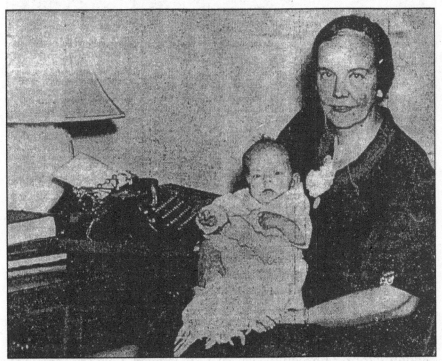

Susan and infant son Albert Alois interviewed by New York reporters in their suite at the Waldorf Astoria, 1936.

Sorrow Inspires Mother To Become Prize Writer

Best Rural Correspondent Visits Here; Tells Views

On Christmas morning, 1932, the year-and-a-half-old daughter of Susan Frawley Eisele died in the tiny town of Blue Earth, Minn.

Mrs. Eisele didn't know it then, but her child's death was to start her on a career which lifted her from obscurity to a position of national prominence as the best country newspaper correspondent in 1936.

Ever since she was 12, she had been "scribbling." She said

Susan and infant son Albert Alois featured in the Washington Herald during the trip to the nation's capital, 1936.

We arrived from Minneapolis by train on Sunday, August 23, and checked into a five-room suite on the fourteenth floor of the Waldorf Astoria Tower. A horde of reporters and photographers from New York's newspapers, wire services and radio networks crowded into our suite to interview my mother, who suddenly found herself a celebrity.[1] However, I was the focus of the article that appeared in *The New York Times* the next day,

WITH A PENNY PENCIL

——— SUSAN FRAWLEY EISELE ———

(The Sentinel is reprinting in whole the threshing time article published in this column last year, a part of which was one of the prize-winning items written by Mrs. Eisele. Requests for the entire article have come from all over the country.)

———o———

THRESHING TIME

Unless you have taken an actual part in the drama of the threshing season, have been one of the characters in this biggest play of the rural year, then you have missed one of life's richest episodes. For into the brocaded fabric of this season is woven and embroidered the most lavish and colorful of all the seasons.

* * *

August 24, 1936, under a one-column, four-deck headline: "RURAL JOURNALIST NOT AWED BY CITY: A BIT STUNNED BY ITS SIZE, BUT SHE FINDS COUNTRY AND URBAN REPORTERS ALIKE; HERE AS A PRIZE WINNER; CORRESPONDENT OF BLUE EARTH, MINN., HAS RECIPE, UNTRIED, FOR STUFFED PEACOCK."

As the *Times* reporter wrote, "Her left arm snug about a seven-week-old baby boy, Mrs. Susan Frawley Eisele of Blue Earth, Minn., picked stoically at a portable typewriter with two fingers of her right hand in her room at the Waldorf-Astoria yesterday. 'Zzklklklklklklklkl, jkjkjkjkjkjkl,' she wrote, for the benefit of photographers. The baby stretched a pink hand toward the white organdy rosette at his mother's black bodice. The last flashlight went off, the camera men said, 'Thank you,' and Mrs. Eisele stopped typing. A friend took the baby, Albert Alois, to its nurse, Mrs. William Hines."

The Herald Tribune's article was accompanied by a three-column photo of her sitting at a portable typewriter while holding me in her lap. (I was "rocked in the only rocking chair in the Waldorf Astoria," she later told readers of her column. "It took him less than a week to become used to city life. Little

---

WITH A PENNY PENCIL
By ALBERT EISELE, Guest Columnist

EDITOR'S NOTE—On August 29, 1936, Albert Eisele, Post Chaise writer was guest columnist for his wife, Mrs. Eisele, who was in Washington. It is one of the best columns that Albert wrote and because of the subject matter contained we are publishing the article.

Albert won the hearts of photographers with wide and ready smiles. A born diplomat, that baby.") *The Sun*, which ran a similar photo, echoed the same theme in its headline and story, as did the *Post*, *World Telegram*, *Evening Journal* and *American*. And the award and news of her celebrity treatment in New York made headlines in newspapers across the country, including her native states of South Carolina and Tennessee.

Speaking with traces of her Southern accent and holding me until I raised a fuss because of the photographers' flashbulbs, she quickly disproved the stereotyped notion of the country journalist. "Someone asked what she thought about rural and urban journalism," the *Times* reported. "'I can't see that there's much difference,' she said. 'You write what you see and we write what we see. Of course, you see a more sophisticated kind of life here; we see the simpler things. But I think we're trying fundamentally to do the same thing. I think that a journalist's highest function is to present life as he sees it.'"

She said her definition of news was not reporting about world events or famous people, but "about the weeds and the crops and the roadsides and the weather and the children," as she had in her prize-winning column, which was about the hard work and shared satisfaction of neighbors helping each other harvest their grain. By drawing material from her life with my father, also a writer, and my two older brothers and the lives of her rural Minnesota neighbors, she said a writer could provide glimpses of truth and beauty by faithfully reporting the reality of everyday life.

For example, she told reporters she was in a café in Blue Earth one day when the town's fire sirens went off, signaling a fire in the country. "I was afraid that something had happened at home," she said. "Then a man came in and said, 'Hell, that's just a farmer's strawstack on fire.' Straw—that's gold to a farmer, it means everything. But a fire in a strawstack wouldn't worry a man in town, just as a fire in town wouldn't worry us in the country. I thought there was a story in that."

She confirmed the Jazz Age image of New Yorkers as popularized by fellow Minnesotan F. Scott Fitzgerald, in an article she later wrote for the *Sentinel*. "Everyone in New York, as far as I can see, smokes and drinks. I never saw a drunken person, but it seems to me that the women particularly try to outdo each other in drinking—they try everything—and seem to get away with it. They smoke almost constantly. No one in New York dresses other than ordinarily. I was disappointed in this because I expected them to be fashion plates."

And she was equally forthright about the city's night life. "The night clubs are night clubs, no fooling. The women there are actually naked, and no illusions. But I think there is more undress on the streets of Blue Earth than New York." Calling the Stork Club "dishwaterish," she told the *Sentinel*. "The Hollywood Night Club on Broadway is supposed to be more representative of the flesh. The chorus girls are beautiful. Girls just like we have in Fairmont and Blue Earth—with maybe a little less on. The jokes are old: just the same kind of jokes as those your husband comes home and tells you—if you let him—after a day at the office, or during threshing."

But when asked in an NBC radio interview what she thought of another Minnesota writer, Sinclair Lewis, and his harsh portrayal of life in small towns like her own, she dismissed him as someone who didn't know his subject. "I liked *Main Street* very much, but that was the last good book Lewis wrote. Novels of small towns or of the farm can only be written by those who live there." And, like many tourists then and now, she found few bargains in New York stores. "It is impossible to shop in New York unless you go for miles to find a reasonable place," she wrote. "I wanted to get a hat there, and went to one of the shops in the Waldorf Astoria, and they had nothing cheaper than $18.50."

My mother assured the assembled reporters that their jobs were safe. "Broadway's lights may be bright and famous, but Mrs. Eisele wouldn't trade her kerosene lamps for all of them," the United Press correspondent wrote. "Neither would she swap jobs with any of New York's newspapermen. Their assignments may cover more sophisticated doings, but to Mrs. Eisele, threshing, fall plowing, cattle slaughtering and lard making, about which she writes, are just as important and not much different." She explained that she had begun writing seriously only four years earlier, as a form of therapy after the death of her two-year-old daughter on Christmas Day 1932, a day after my brother was born, and that she and her husband both wrote in the light of a kerosene lamp after putting their children to bed. "That makes as good a light as your electricity, and I wouldn't trade," she said.

The Herald Tribune described her as "a plain but exceedingly intelligent women," while the *Times* wrote an editorial declaring that she "has defined the profession of journalism in words that will make all good newspaper men proud." However, the *Times* also challenged her view that a journalist's "highest function is to present life as he sees it," declaring that "The newspaper man should be content to describe the things that he sees. There is a big difference between what a man sees and 'as' he sees it."

During a weeklong visit, she paid a call on Mayor Fiorello LaGuardia in the summer City Hall in the Bronx; had tea with President Franklin Roosevelt's daughter Anna at the New York Democratic Women's headquarters; sat beside the presiding judge at a session of the city's Night Court; and met renowned industrial designer Donald Deskey, a native of Blue Earth, whose art deco street lamps adorned many New York streets, including one across from City Hall.[2]

"Mayor Yearns to Be Columnist," the American reported above a three-column photo of LaGuardia presenting my mother with a five-foot-long pencil in recognition of her column, called "With a Penny Pencil," which he offered to guest edit. And he told her he was sorry he couldn't go to Minnesota for the funeral of Governor Floyd B. Olson, who had just died. "Governor Olson was one of the outstanding progressives the country, and we have been friends for many years. The nation has lost of one of its great leaders." And when my mother complained that she had seen few babies in New York, LaGuardia replied, "Oh, we have plenty of babies. That is one thing we haven't any depression on." My mother later said she had seldom taken a liking to any man as she had to him. "Mayor LaGuardia is outspoken, sincere, genial and altogether a nice man. The world needs more men like him."

Although disappointed by the gothic vastness of St. Patrick's Cathedral, where her immigrant Irish father worshipped on his arrival in this country in 1888, she called the

Cathedral of St. John the Divine "a gorgeous church." And while she was unimpressed by the Stork Club or Jack Dempsey's restaurant, which she compared to "being in a pool room or barber shop—uncomfortable for a woman," she was thrilled by her first sight of the Statue of Liberty from the Staten Island ferry, and by New York itself. Despite the city's "metallic soul," she found it "bigger and more wonderful than I ever dreamed of."

Nevertheless, she echoed the classic judgment of many first-time visitors to New York, saying, "But I wouldn't want to live here. I have my inspirations from the soil, and I have to stay there to get them."

My mother's visit attracted the attention of syndicated columnists Walter Winchell, Westbrook Pegler, and Dorothy Kilgallen, who devoted entire columns to her. Pegler wrote that the big city reporters were surprised to find that "she is neither illiterate nor a wide-eyed and somewhat apprehensive Aunt Samanthy in a sunbonnet, afraid to leave her hotel on account of 'them white-slavers who lurk in every New York doorway waiting to snatch a country girl to a fate which is worse than death.'" Noting that the same prize had gone to a rural Missouri woman the year before, Pegler commented, "Two years running, now, country ladies have come to New York to be astonished, and neither one has attempted to blow out the electric light. Possibly both of them, when they were let alone at night, turned to the Wall Street closing prices to see what was doing today."

Like Kilgallen, Winchell not only wrote a laudatory column but invited my mother to author a guest column, which she did a few weeks later. In it, she called the New York journalists "as fine a group of men as I have ever met." She added, "This, above all, endeared New York to me. I formerly had the small town idea of metropolitan newspaper men: hard-boiled, heartless, nervy people who pried into private affairs and broke hearts and laughed at you behind your back. Well, they weren't like that at all."

In his column, Winchell agreed with my mother's assertion that "reporting here and in the sticks is essentially the same." But he advised her "of the opportunities and evils she'd be up against" if she ever decided to "transfer her portable to the local city rooms. . . . This burg offers the best opportunities, coin and adventure of any, but it also ranks high in double-crossings, headaches, and disappointments." He added, "One of the grandest things about New York, Mrs. Eisele, is that every once in a while a yarn breaks that gives each paper a chance to turn a reporter loose on some big time writing. As happened the other day when Peter, the bear, broke out of the zoo and had to be shot. Every rag had a piece on the incident, which has this reporter scattering orchids to the authors of all of them." Winchell said he agreed completely with my mother's statement that "a journalist's highest function is to present life as he sees it," adding in words that any present-day journalist probably would agree with: "Very well said. But the trouble is too many readers want you to see it their way."

When Winchell died in 1971, my mother recalled her encounter with him. "He was at that time the nation's top columnist and radio commentator. One day he called my hotel and asked me for an interview. I just about fell over and so did my sponsors. But I knew Winchell was a gossip columnist and my presence there was that of a Midwestern farm woman who was neither glamorous nor material for him, I thought. All I wrote about was setting hens and life on a small farm, so I wondered if he was going to make fun of me or slay me with his sharp tongue and pen." But she was pleasantly surprised. "I shouldn't have been so suspicious," she wrote in her "Countryside" column. "Walter Winchell and I fell in love with each other from the moment we met. In his syndicated column in a New York newspaper the following Sunday, he gave me the whole column. After the interview, he told me to keep being myself, not to let anyone make me over, and that he envied me my humdrum life. So I think his advice to me could be followed by everybody. You only fool yourself when you try to create a false image, or cover yourself with veneer, or pretend."

From New York, she and I went on to Washington, where my mother was supposed to meet President Roosevelt, who, ironically, had gone to Minnesota to attend the funeral of Governor Olson, the radical, flamboyant and controversial three-term governor who was planning to run for the U.S. Senate when he died of cancer at age forty-five. But she got the star treatment there as well. *The Washington Times-Herald* ran a page one story with a photograph of her holding me while reading Winchell's column in the *Herald*, under the headline, "Sorrow Inspires Mother to Become Prize Writer: Best Rural Correspondent Visits Here; Tells Views." I also made my first visit to the White House, strolling through the gates, unchallenged, with my nurse pushing me in a stroller. "Mrs. Hines was wheeling you around while I was doing something else, and she came to the White House and the gates were open, probably because President Roosevelt wasn't there, so she went in," she later told me. "She got up to the front portico and was looking around when some security guards rushed up and asked what she was doing. She said the gates were open so she went in. They said that was the first time this had ever happened, and asked her to leave."[3]

After returning home, my mother wrote a thirteen-part series about her trip for the *Minneapolis Journal* in which she expressed her admiration of the nation's capital, as well as her ambivalence. She wrote that she was deeply impressed by the White House and Capitol building and the city's monuments, but declared, "Washington is not a city. It is the soul of America clothed in white marble flesh." And she assured her readers that her baby son was pleased with his visit to Gotham as well. "The baby likes New York fine. He is gaining rapidly on pasteurized milk that costs us . . . almost a dollar a quart. And then he isn't satisfied." She added that he became famous for being rocked to sleep in the Waldorf-Astoria's only rocking chair, and that a Pullman porter on the train home called him "one of the most travelingest babies in the world."

While she was gone, Wheeler McMillan wrote her "Penny Pencil" column, and delivered his judgment about her. "With graciousness and ease, she has met famous people—and impressed them," he wrote. "Some New York reporters came expecting to meet a funny person from the back country, who could be kidded for the amusement of metropolitan readers. They talked with her and went back and wrote friendly stories of a fellow worker, whom they had found to be well-poised, well-dressed and well-bred. They liked the intelligence, patience, and straightforwardness with which she answered their questions. Even the photographers, those hard-boiled masters of impertinence, were polite and considerate."

She never got over her love affair with New York. In the guest column she wrote for Winchell, she said, "Before my trip east, I thought that inhabitants of New York would be in some strange, ineffable way, different from small town dwellers. I was mistaken and disappointed. I found you folks to be pretty much like the folks here at home or in Minneapolis. I had expected New York to be plainly tattooed upon its inhabitants. But it wasn't. And try as I would, I never discovered the mark. You were gentle, conservative, cultured, alert, discerning, sympathetic—just like next door neighbors.

"But find New York, its significance and its essence, we did, Mr. Winchell. Otherwise, it wouldn't have made sense. Your skyscrapers are New York. They are the cathedrals of commerce and industry in which your city worships. They are beautiful, inspiring and siren-like. No wonder you love New York. I was coming back from Staten Island . . . and suddenly that exquisite skyline of yours broke into view! Shameful sentimentalist that I am, I felt like going down on my knees at the sight—and thanking God that He made men with intellect and vision strong enough to conceive such magnificent architecture. For certainly, the skyscraper represents man's material progress in exactly the same way that the cathedral represents his spiritual progress.

"And now that I have caught the real spirit of New York, I love it, too, and it seems to belong to me as well as to you, Mr. Winchell. That is how it should be. New York should belong to the whole United States, not just to New Yorkers. We should be proud of it and it should be Our City, as London is to England, and Paris is to France. No sectionalism or jealousy should deprive the citizens of this country from pointing with pride to this wonder city of yours and ours. It can never be overshadowed or duplicated."

In her final article for the *Journal*, however, she proved she hadn't been seduced by the bright lights and famous people in New York and Washington. "In the East, we

Midwesterners are regarded with amazement," she wrote. "It is hard for them to realize that we are the same people that they are. That we dress, live, act and think just like they do. Only we are more leisurely about it. We seem to have a longer day here. Sometimes we think Easterners regard us a people living in a far-away land. We, the people of the Midwest, are going to have to sell our country to the East. With our fertile fields and lovely scenery and composite population, we have a combination that will stand up against anything any time."

My mother, who never returned to New York or Washington, never forgot her brush with fame but tried to keep it in perspective and learn from Winchell's sage advice. In 1975, she summed up her experience in New York and its lesson in a letter to my then-twelve-year-old daughter Kitty: "I felt right at home in New York and loved it and still do. I saw the Bowery and Chinatown and most of the seamy side of New York as well as the gilded. I met all the celebrities and famous news people and such, and I was wined and dined. I tried to be myself and not attempt to put on a false front and it seemed to go over big. Maybe that is the way we should always act. I found out that the higher up a person is, the more approachable he is."

But she proved badly mistaken when asked by reporters on that day in August 1936, what her baby son would be when he grew up. "Little Albert, she promised, would not be a writer," the *Herald Tribune* reported. "I'll be satisfied to make a good plain dirt farmer out of him. I don't want him ever to get the writer's itch."

Notes

[1] All were friendly except for one, Cornelius Vanderbilt, but he wrote a gracious story for Hearst.

[2] Deskey, who left Blue Earth in 1912, returned for his high school reunion in 1962. But he didn't have fond memories of his hometown, telling a newspaper reporter that he had a miserable childhood with no close friends and was bullied in school. In 2013, after learning that many of the deteriorating Deskey street lamps were being replaced, the author had one shipped to Blue Earth, where it was installed on Main Street.

[3] My next visit to the White House came twenty-seven years later, in October, 1965, while covering a presidential press conference as a Washington correspondent for the St. Paul Dispatch & Pioneer Press, and security was considerably tighter.

Chapter Six

Commonweal and Countryside

THE FIFTEEN YEARS between my mother's trip to New York and Washington and my father's fatal diagnosis of cancer were the happiest and most productive of their lives as they combined farming and writing while raising a family. She continued her prize-winning "Penny Pencil" column, and he continued writing his "Post Chaise" column while producing the short stories that would earn him the Catholic literary community's recognition and respect. He also worked on a novel that was never published. And in 1940, they began jointly writing a column called "Countryside" for the *Blue Earth Post*, which billed it as "America's Most Authentic Farm Column." It was so well-received that they syndicated it and sold it to some thirty newspapers in Minnesota, South Dakota, and Iowa.

As she told one of those papers, the *Mason City* (Iowa) *Globe Gazette*, which wrote a lengthy feature article on my parents in November 1941, only days before the attack on Pearl Harbor, "We started writing about farm life, the thing we know most about. It seems to be a field that has just been scratched. Now that we have found that rural writing is in demand and that it is growing in popularity, we are devoting

Joe with dog Trixie and brothers Albert Alois (center) and Arnold, about 1941.

all our time to it—that is, our writing time." The Mason City paper's article, headlined "Albert and Susan Eisele and Their Friendly Farm Philosophy," featured photos of my father "working on a battered old Oliver typewriter" and my mother working at her coal-fired stove, along with sidebars and photos of me and my two brothers with Trixie, our dog, and another on Joe and the Spotted Poland China pig he showed at the Faribault County fair.

And in 1949, she began writing a column for *The Witness* newspaper in Dubuque, Iowa, that was originally called

Susan does double duty while writing and cooking.

"Jottings of a Farmer's Wife" and later "Pocketful of Pencils," and a joint women's column with Florence Hynes Willette for the Knights of Columbus magazine Columbia, which she continued writing for the rest of her life. And both my parents remained actively involved in farm, business and professional organizations as well as the Catholic Church.

My father had always dreamed of becoming a writer, as was clear in a remarkable memo I found

JOTTINGS OF THE
FARMER'S WIFE

Susan Frawley Eisele

Cat keeps Albert company while he writes his "Post Chaise" column.

among his papers. The memo is undated but probably was written sometime in the early 1940s, after his first stories were published. I don't know whom he addressed it to but I suspect it was to an editor considering one of his stories, or perhaps the editor of one of the anthologies in which his articles appeared: "At the age of about fifteen, feeling the need

BLUE EARTH POST, BLUE EARTH, MINNESOTA

THE POST CHAISE - ALBERT EISELE

The Japs opened their war on America in typical Japanese fash-

thur was taken by the Japs, but only after an unparalleled and

the Russo naval ba Straits. I seiged Po sent their to the Far preparatio sing half of expression, I set out to be a cartoonist," he wrote. "After a couple of years of this effort, I decided that the heavy work of farming was not conducive to the drawing of a perfect line, and so I switched to writing."

He noted that his first published work had appeared in a Catholic newspaper in Iowa in 1919. "I wrote stories in the O. Henry fashion, a number of which were preserved in all their horror on the Young People's Page of the *Catholic Daily Tribune* of Dubuque, Iowa," he recalled. "I broke away, finally, from my imitations of O. Henry, and began writing as I really wanted to write, in which I tried to express myself in my own way. It was not until 1937 that my first magazine story was published. . . . Since I began my writing efforts in 1913, this means that I wrote for twenty-four years before finally getting into magazine print. What sustained me through those long years of rejection slips? I think it was the firm belief that I had something to give to the world, something definite that I wasn't finding in the stuff that I was reading in those days, in the best magazines. Of the stories that I read in those struggling years, I liked best those of Ruth Suckow; I found them artistic and true to life, but I was convinced that she was not making the best use of her material, that really I was closer to the soil than she was, and that I was in position to turn out some credible stories of my own."[1]

His first short story, titled "Day of Leisure," appeared in *The Catholic World* in June 1937 (his first poem, titled "Harvest Moment," had appeared in *Spirit* magazine two years earlier). It proved to be a breakthrough. In the next sixteen years, before his untimely death in 1951, he would publish some eighty short stories in other mostly Catholic literary journals such as *America, Ave Maria, The Commonweal,*

Land and Home, Spirit, The Torch, St. Anthony's Messenger,
and *The Sign,* along with more than 100 unpublished short
stories.[2] And more than two dozen of his poems would appear
in *Spirit* and *The Ave Maria* and other magazines, while he
wrote dozens more that weren't published, either because
they were rejected or he didn't submit them to a publisher.

But he decided that the best medium for him was not
poetry but fiction, in the form of the short story. In November
1937, he sold a second story to *The Commonweal.* Called "The
Toss-up," it was about a tenant farmer and his demanding
and unforgiving landlord and was the first of some sixteen of
his stories to appear in that magazine.[3] "He was a genius of
the short story," my mother later declared. "He had thousands of notes and said he never used the same one twice. He
was paid as much as $200 an article."

It was another of his stories, "The Brother Who Came,"
(*See* pp. 130-135, and on p. 130)in the February 10, 1939, issue
of *The Commonweal* that put him on the Catholic literary map.
Described by David Marshall, a Fordham professor and founder
of the literary magazine *A.D.,* as "one of the finest short stories
ever written." The story was about a poor South Dakota farmer
named Steve who came to his sister-in-law's funeral in Minnesota, while two well-to-do brothers failed to come from Wisconsin and New Jersey. After the funeral, Peter, the bereaved
husband, tearfully thanked his brother and asked him to wait
until the next morning to start his long drive home in his old
car. But Steve insisted that he leave in case it snowed, then
broke down while confessing that he couldn't afford to bring his
whole family because of seven years of crop failure. The story
ends as Peter watches his brother's departure: ". . . and when
the car had mounted to the brow of a distant rise there was a

backfire of the motor that threw out a shawl of sparks. Then the car disappeared below the hill, and only the stars above remained." However, the story also displays what he later identified as one of his shortcomings, which was the use of big words—such as "claquer," "corroborator" and "celestial"—which he said he used to compensate for his lack of a high school and college education—as well as a lot of unnecessary dialogue.

In 1946, in *Ariston*, a literary magazine published by the College of Saint Catherine in St. Paul, Lorraine Guerber, a student from Blue Earth, wrote of "The Brother Who Came," "the reader is stirred when the bereaved Peter Roth, whose wife has just died, clasps his brother Steve and says, 'Steve, I'm so glad you came! You were the only one of my people . . .' The reader cannot help but being comforted with the grateful Peter who thanks his brother over and over again . . . when Steve himself had so many sorrows in the guise of crop failures. This genuine act of love meant so much to Peter, whose wealthy brothers did not bother to come."

"The Brother Who Came" was among a half dozen of his stories chosen for publication in literary anthologies. It was one of twenty-eight included in "Our Father's House," published by Sheed and Ward in 1945 and edited by Sister Mariella Gable, a Benedictine nun at the College of Saint Benedict in Minnesota. She described her choices—Leo Tolstoy, Sean O'Faolain, Steven Vincent Benet, Brendan Gill, and J.F. Powers—as authors of some of "the best short stories that have dealt directly with eternal verities or with the local color of Catholic life" (although she cautioned, "May no one call them Catholic stories"). She said of my father's work, "His art is stark, stripped. What he has to say is truth seen so clearly that it surprises. He writes of the ancient verities.

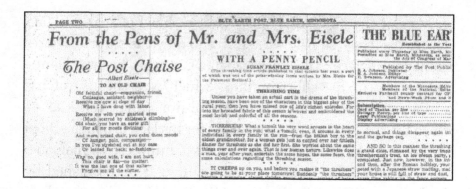

About them clings the odor of the soil."

Although my father was reluctant to reveal his feelings, most of his fiction was based on himself and his personal experiences. Almost all of his stories were set in the rural landscape he knew so well, and its characters were based on himself or derived from the people he'd encountered or knew. For example, in his story, "Anniversary" (*The Commonweal*, July 1, 1938), a farmer named Vincent has just managed to pay off the chattel mortgage that hung over his head, and his wife and three children, since the Great Depression. But he still considers himself a failure because he hasn't been able to buy the farm he is renting or buy a tractor. But as he works his fields one day, he suddenly realizes that "the work he had done that afternoon was good," and he is not a failure. "The revelation of it all flooded his mind and his being—he was reassured; and grateful, too, that economic concern could not at all times blind one to the value of essential things."

Or "Molasses Sam" in the March 1942 issue of the National Catholic Rural Life Conference magazine *Land and Home*, about a slowpoke but good-natured farmer helping to move his neighbor. Or "The Thimblers" (*Ave Maria*, May 25, 1946) in which a woman's preparations to entertain her sewing club kept her husband busy wallpapering, painting and repairing the chicken house. Or "The Serving Committee" in the April 1948 issue of *The Sign*, in which a rich farmer refuses to join the men of his parish on a committee conducting a card party to benefit starving people because he doesn't want to wash dirty dishes. He ridicules the man who is cleaning up after the party, who turns out to be a saintly figure who feeds and washes the feet of an old hobo.

After his initial successes, he published four stories in 1938 and an average of five in each of the succeeding years until his death in 1951, including nine in 1945 and 1948, In addition to "The Brother Who Came," several others were selected for anthologies: 'The Farewell Party," (*The Catholic World*, April 1938) was included in *Pilgrims All* in 1943; "The Dance" (*The Commonweal*, June 4, 1943) in *The Commonweal Reader* in 1949; "Farmer at Forty Hours" (*Ave Maria*, January 1, 1944), in *The Catholic Digest Reader* in 1952; and "Easter Duty" (*America*, April 22, 1944) in *Their Country's Pride* in 1948. Also, his story "The Penitential Garb" (*America*, January 18, 1947) was reprinted in *The Catholic Digest*, as was "All the Parades" (*America*, January 1, 1949).

In April 1945, Monsignor Luigi Ligutti, executive secretary of the National Catholic Rural Life Conference, whose magazine, *Land and Soil*, had published several of his stories, wrote "My dear Albert: This letter is written so as to make your wife jealous. I have just read your very fine story, 'The Money Tree.' It's the finest recipe for a rural pastor. It ought to be read on Sunday mornings." He added, "We need some more stories from your pen for *Land and Soil*. Shag some down this way. These are great days in which to write stories, while out in the field plowing or planting." The qualities of the story that Monsignor Liguitti cited were evident in all of his short stories, and his newspaper columns as well.

As Lorraine Guerber wrote in the College of St. Catherine magazine in 1946, "Albert Eisele is not a 'gentleman' farmer. He plows his fields in the fall and spring; he plants his crops and harvests them. Evenings and in between times he writes. With a pad and pencil in his pocket always, he manages to find in the unsophisticated everyday happenings vast material for writing. His settings are the cornfields and green pastures, the machinery-cluttered farmyard with its paint-chipped buildings, the dusty road to town. His characters are people like 'Susan and the boys,' people like his neighbors—tobacco-chewing farmers and their young children—the district school teacher just out of normal school, the parish priest in town. His stories aren't spectacular—just the daily lives of people like these. . . . The old bachelor-farmer of 'Easter Duty,' who hated women and might have been one of Albert's neighbors. The reader senses his sympathetic understanding of the sinner and gives thanks with him at the man's final repentance." Guerber cited several of his short stories, such as "The Exorcism" in the October 6, 1945 issue of *America*, and "The Farewell Party" in the April 1938 issue of *The Catholic World*. "In 'Exorcism' this same deep regard for Faith shines through the virtuous carpenter and the futile devilish attempt of the employer to tempt him. His stories are simple, edifying, but never preachy. Some, like 'The Farewell Party' take a humorous turn."

But perhaps the best critique of my father's short stories appeared in the *Saint Benedict's Quarterly* a year after his death, and deserves to be quoted at length. Noting that he had "showed much promise in the field of Catholic fiction (and) died just as he was beginning to achieve a name in the literary world," Mary Agnes O'Hern wrote. "Eisele's fiction stands as a sharp silhouette against the work of the sentimental writers. He wrote about people who were not unlike himself. These people lived on farms and knew God's creation only as those who live so near to nature can. His people are not victims of social problems but are mature, responsible personalities whom Eisele offers an opportunity to reveal their emotions in a colorful, rustic setting."

O'Hern, a St. Benedict's graduate, looked at several of his best-known stories. "His characterization is so life-like that the people in the stories are brought very close to the readers. This effect if brought about through the externals of choice dialogue and action. In 'The Snowstorm,' the reader feels a penetrating sympathy for Edward, the leading character, when he realizes that he has committed a mortal sin:

> And when he was ready for bed he knelt down frankly and asked God to forgive him for the mortal sin he had committed by looking at, and lusting after a woman. He had looked at her not for a fleeting moment but for many full moments; he had looked at her intently and doggedly; had been beset by every impure thought and desire and had not only been beset by them but had welcomed them. Then there was no question but that his soul was not in mortal sin.

O'Hern called my father's fictional creations "the little people of life, who so often turn out to be the big people. Something upsets their stream of simple rural life, which makes for complications. Through the complication they find something new planted in their souls." Such was the case, she wrote, with another leading character named Edward in "The Burial of Max Phillips" (*The Commonweal*, March 14, 1941). Through witnessing two burials, he feels he is brought

closer to life. He went to the cemetery to pay his respects
to the body of a neighbor, Max Philips, who had not regularly practiced his [Catholic] religion. Edward couldn't
help noticing that there were no relatives but only other
neighbors . . . It was then that he was distracted by sobs
of grieved parents as they watched the priest bless the
coffin of their young boy in a nearby plot. There was no
one left to pray for poor Max who needed prayers . . .

She compared my father's style to Russian writers like
Chekov, "stark, realistic and powerful, and said it succeeded
"because it never retards the movement of the story. Eisele
in one simple sentence can make the reader feel an aging
farmer's futile attempt to hold back the passing years. 'It was
always on the opening days of field work that one realized
that another year had passed, that the gray of one more year
had come into one's hair.'" Like Chekov, "he uses only one
dramatic situation. He presents a problem rather than re-
solves it. The writer describes the circumstances of origina-
tion, pointing out psychological or other forces involved on
either side. . . . The emotional effect is powerful and significant to the reader. In his stories the far results of things are
hidden from us, as so often happens in real life. The story
ends before the problem is solved, but the relations of the
characters are defined well enough to predict the outcome."

For example, the reader of "Cities and Stones" (*The
Commonweal*, August 12, 1949) knows that the protagonist
Chad Galbrath "will be strong enough to overcome his fear of
talking about his war experiences. His family wanted to hear
about his bombing raids, but he always avoided it with, 'Oh,
I don't know. There isn't much to tell.'" But as he blasted
rocks from the fields for fall plowing, he noticed that his horse
ran away from the noise of the explosion. "And the story ends

with Chad remarking, 'That's a funny thing about Old Belle. Yesterday she was grazing and saw me blast that rock. It scared her I guess, and today she's still scared."

Finally, O'Hern offered "The Dance" (*The Commonweal*, June 4, 1943) as an example of how my father could "make a single image more saturated with life than whole chapters in a book." Quoting from his description of a farmer tilling his field, she wrote, "Bits of shattered cornstalks flew about, some striking against the disk with a musical sound, suggestive of a xylophone, and others flying in Vincent's face like bat-fowled sparrows." And she called attention to his description of nature, and its ability to alert the ears. "The setting sun was blanketed with a bank of clouds and flashes of lightning showed far in the background. The fields of oats, fully headed but not yet ripened, shone in the shadowed

Susan and Albert enjoy time together with the boys and dog Trixie on the farm, about 1945.

evening with a bluish sheen. . . . The sound of illegal pheasant shooting was in the air. . . . Tractors were modern and frogs age-old, but the voices of the two blended with a mystic beauty that lay upon the rural world like benediction,

O'Hern concluded, "Albert Eisele is definitely a literary craftsman. His stories pull the gauze from the wound and expose the naked wound. It is often through the art of implication that he accomplishes this effective way of presenting truth. Due to the skill of implication, Eisele earns a coveted place in the hierarchy of Catholic fiction."

But my father was no stranger to rejection. Many of his stories were turned down by the editors of *Commonweal*, *America*, and other magazines before he either rewrote them or found editors who liked them. In February 1948, for example, Father Harold Gardiner, S.J., the literary editor of *America*, which had already published a half-dozen of his stories, rejected one of his stories called "The Snowstorm" after another editor agreed with him "that a great number of our readers would be almost certain to get a wrong impression from the article. That impression would be that neither the author nor the editors of *America* knew much about moral theology." He said my father failed to "make it clear that we would not be agreeing with the rather shaky moral theology" of the main character, "who sees mortal sins everywhere." (However, *A.D.*, a new magazine, published the story in December 1950.) In March 1949, Fr. Gardiner turned down another story, declaring that "Your newest concoction, as you call it, doesn't strike me as up to your level. The tone is good but I think the point that the priest makes which sways your choirmaster isn't quite convincing." He suggested my father rewrite and re-submit the story, called "The New Choir." I don't know if he rewrote it but he then sent it to a magazine called *The Christian Family*, which promptly accepted it.

In August 1940, Edward Skillen, editor of *The Commonweal*, which had already published four of his stories, wrote that his story "The Visit" was "both too simple and too sentimental . . . in that it makes out Edgar's plight far worse that it actually is when you consider how many other displaced farmers and their families are on the road." And when he sent stories to non-Catholic magazines, he usually was rejected, as when Arnold Gingrich, editor of *Esquire*, returned his 1944 story about a farm sale with a curt comment, "Not a usable tale or style."

Even Eve Woodburn, the New York literary agent he hired, was not helpful in selling his short stories or his novel. In April 1948, referring to one of his short stories, she wrote, "I read 'The Fast Horse' with a great deal of interest, but I felt that the story built up to a lecture. . . . While the story had excellent suspense, I felt that it dragged considerably and could have been told in a much faster tempo. Too many bits and too many scenes. . . . This really does slow up your story." And in July, she wrote, "I'm truly sorry we have to return 'The Artist' to you but I don't believe I can place it." Noting that it had been rejected by *Argosy*, *Colliers*, *This Week*, and *Country Gentleman*, she told him, "Your motivation is weak. Watch out for motivation. It is the 'why' of a story, in other words, why did it all happen and if the motivation is weak the plot is bound to be weak." She encouraged him to send other stories but he seems to have given up on her as I found no other correspondence with her in his files.

But my father's greatest disappointment probably was his failure to publish his novel about a German immigrant farmer in the 1890s entitled *The Yoke of Honey*, that he had been working on for many years, and which he intended to be the first book of a trilogy. He was encouraged after Father Joseph Husslein, S.J., the editor-in-chief of Milwaukee-based Bruce Publishing Company's Religion and Cultural series, read the manuscript and praised it. In a May 5, 1942, letter, he called it "pure, wholesome and perfectly conformable to Catholic teaching and ideals. It is well written, with interesting character drawings and colorful nature descriptions. I have found it to be pleasant reading, while it conveys its lessons with directness." However, Father Husslein suggested a new title—he favored "The Yoke of Cana"—but said his real problem was not the title but with his prospective audience. "There are about a half dozen messages which are innocent in themselves, but which quite likely may suffice to exclude the book from high school and college libraries, he wrote. "I am not finicky, I am merely indicating a problem which any publisher would have to face in bringing the book to our Catholic young people."

Taking Father Husslein's advice that young Catholics might react to his novel, my father revised his manuscript and submitted it to Bruce Publishing, which liked it but had additional reservations. One editor, Robert Broderick, cautioned him against including "too much of the bickering of daily life lest you give your characters a shrewish twist in the reader's mind." So my father revised the manuscript yet again. But on May 13, 1943, Editor William Bruce informed him that his readers reacted unfavorably to the revised manuscript, saying, "In fact, we believe that the book is not as good in its present form as it was in the original manuscript." Although he offered to bring my father to Milwaukee do discuss his concerns, Father decided against going and instead began an extensive correspondence with the publisher. On May 1, 1944, Robert Broderick of the publisher's editorial department, explained his main concern in a three-page letter, which he said "is best summed up in the phrase that you have stylistic difficulty which, in turn, falls into a plotting difficulty." He followed up with a two-page letter and nine pages of suggested changes in the first two chapters, but my father apparently concluded that he should forget about writing novels and do what he did best, write short stories.

In September 1944, the *Minneapolis Sunday Tribune* featured my parents and family in a full-page article that included photographs of my mother at her typewriter "in the kitchen in an atmosphere of pots and pans" and my father working on "an old Oliver typewriter in his book-lined study in the living room." There were also photos of them picking corn, feeding chickens and hogs and of me and my brother Arnold gathering the mail while on horseback. "Farming is much more than a hard-won livelihood (but) also a beautiful and exciting experience and the source of inspiration for their avocation—writing, more than 5,000 words a week in columns for twenty-six newspapers," the paper reported.

"Most widely circulated of their columns is 'Countryside,'" which they write together. In it they record the simple doings of everyday rural life, emphasizing its beauty and more significant details." The newspaper added that my mother was "city-bred and holder of a law degree" to whom "words come quickly and easily," while my father "writes slowly and painstakingly, making liberal use of his carefully classified files of ideas that come to him while he is milking, working in the fields or reading."

In retrospect, my mother may have been referring to her husband as well of herself in a "Penny Pencil" column at the time. "Why is a literary ability often unrecognized?" she wondered. "Or why, too, does one have to struggle along alone, perhaps for years before receiving recognition? The answer must be searched for where one generally goes last to find the answer: in one's own heart. Struggle for recognition often becomes motivating impulse. A writer thinks only of eventual success. This deflects the mind from its real and original purpose—that of creating literature. . . . If only one's literary growth or creative ability could be remembered as the ultimate goal, and the recognition and remuneration be considered as only lesser goals, then the complexity would vanish."

Notes

[1]Ruth Suckow was an Iowa writer whose fictional depictions of rural life prompted H.L. Mencken to call her "America's most important female writer." She died in 1960 at the age of sixty-seven. Ironically, one of her stories appeared in *Their Country's Pride*, the same 1948 literary anthology as one of my father's. It was about an Iowa farmer's wife who underwent an examination at the Mayo Clinic. But unlike my father's fatal cancer diagnosis in 1951, she only had to have her gallbladder removed, and she recovered. A further irony was that the anthology's ecclesiastical censor was Msgr. Max Satory, who later was the pastor at Blue Earth who administered the last rites to my father.

[2]Some of his best short stories and my mother's columns are attached, beginning on page 126.

[3]The Jesuit magazine *America* and the National Catholic Rural Life Conference magazine *Land and Home*, each published ten of his short stories.

Chapter Seven

The Diary

M Y FATHER WAS A ROBUST MAN who had enjoyed good health for most of his fifty-four years and clearly expected to live to an old age. In fact, only three years earlier, in 1948, he had undergone a complete checkup at the Mayo Clinic in Rochester—mostly because my mother insisted on it after he had some stomach upsets and her sister was a nurse there—and was given a clean bill of health. "My doctor said my Rochester trip was not necessary and that my condition, which he said was a spastic stomach, could be controlled or cured," he wrote in a diary he began in March, 1951 —which is the most informative and poignant document among his papers and which the rest of this chapter is taken from. "They told me the same thing at Mayo's and it cleared up as they said it would when I stopped trying to do too much field work and too much writing at the same time."

But both his farming and writing were going well. My older brother, Joe, who was waiting to be called to military service, was helping run the farm, and magazine editors were asking my father for more articles and short stories, and he had almost completed a novel. Calling my mother up to his study, which was lined with clipboards holding finished or nearly finished short stories, he told her that Catholic magazines had just accepted two of them, accompanied by substantial checks. "From now on, the going will be easier," he assured her. "She looked out the window and said, in what now seems an almost clairvoyant way, 'But, Albert, we aren't getting any younger. Why don't you get busy on that novel and get it done?' I assured her blithely, I'll live to be a hundred! 'I hope you do,' she replied not so blithely."

A few days later, he drove her to Mankato to catch a train to Tennessee for a brother's funeral, and as they said goodbye, she told him he looked younger and better that he'd looked in years. "That made me feel fine. She wouldn't have said it if she hadn't meant it. I drove back to the farm over drifted roads, and outside of the fact that I missed her, and that my heart was heavy because soon our oldest son would be leaving for the Army, I felt deeply happy. I plunged into a short story that night and completed it and mailed it out."

But he felt "strange" the next morning. "It was as if a great depression had suddenly come upon me," he wrote in the ninety-page diary that chronicled the last nine months of his life, and was finished by my mother. "I no longer felt the desire to live. I was weary. I was frightened. Never before in my life had I felt like this. . . . So I went up to see our parish priest, Father Max Satory. I went twice to see him, but he wasn't home. I don't know why I went to him instead of my doctor, except that I somehow felt insecure of everything, the here, the hereafter." Then he went to a doctor, telling him of his depression. After examining him, the doctor said there was nothing he could put his finger on, and he returned home, convinced that he could "lick this thing."

A few days later, when my mother called from Tennessee, he found that he "couldn't even talk to her in the old, familiar way. It was as if I was talking to a stranger. I felt terrible about it, and she tried to find out what was wrong. . . . I know I hurt her but I didn't have the will to even talk. She hung up, puzzled, I know, and said she was coming right back. The next day, she called me from Chicago, but I was still in this strange, unresponsive condition, I wanted to reassure her everything was fine but everything wasn't fine, and I was torn between the desire to pretend it was and to make myself believe that I was just imagining things. Another snowstorm came and Arnold and I drove the forty-five miles to Mankato, and her train was late. It was the first time in my life that I hadn't been there eagerly awaiting her return. This time I sat in the back seat and let Arnold go to meet his mother. I didn't have the strength to go. I felt like an old man. Something awful had happened to me in the last few days. Susan tried to assure me that whatever was the matter, it would be all right. 'No matter what it is, physical, spiritual, financial or whatever, together we'll work it out,' she said in her characteristic way."

But it wasn't, even though he had two more short stories accepted in May, and he felt that after years of trying, he had at last gotten the hang of it. "Then, late that month, a kind of weariness began showing up in me. I didn't want to get out of bed, and when I did, I was tired. For years I'd gotten up with the dawn and done my writing, then I'd make coffee and bring Susan a cup. But now I wouldn't have minded having her bring me coffee in bed. I would wake up with my pajamas wet and my pillow soaked. She took my temperature and told me I should go to the doctor, but I stalled until July 26, and she got me to consent. . . . When we got to the doctor's

87

office, I asked her if she wanted to go into the consultation office with me, and she said she didn't, she just wanted to make sure that I didn't change my mind and go down to the pool hall instead for a game of snooker."

Yet, after a week of tests, doctors couldn't pinpoint the problem, but they "knew something was very wrong," and suggested he go to the Mayo Clinic in Rochester. Again, he resisted but finally gave in to my mother's importuning, and they made the 115-mile trip in September, with my mother driving. On September 7, a young doctor examined him and found a tender spot near his right kidney. And another young doctor did the same, with the same result. They ordered further tests, including x-rays, and on the afternoon of September 10, he and my mother met with the senior doctor handling his case, who told them the x-rays showed an enlarged right kidney. When he said "it was a very serious condition," my father asked him to "please give us the truth. We can stand it. Is the enlargement of a malignant nature?" The doctor said he believed it was and when asked if there was any hope of cure, "he shook his head gloomily and in silence." Then my mother asked, "in a tone of voice that she might have used in inquiring how far it was to the next town," if the kidney could be removed. "Not any more," the doctor said. "The lungs are involved. The cancer is in his blood and has spread to his lungs. That accounts for his coughing and fever." He told my parents that my father probably had a year to live, at the most.

As my father wrote in his diary, "We had asked for the truth, and we had gotten it. We appreciate Dr. D's frankness. No beating round the bush, no subterfuges, no having to wonder, no having to pretend. This way Susan and I could meet our adversary in the open. It was better than making up little white lies. She wouldn't now have to look away instead of being able to look me clearly, and I wouldn't have to be puzzled and wondering about my true condition." Arnold appeared, ready to take his parents back and to bring them home. "And my mother told him they'd gotten a bad report. She tried to break it gently but in a way she did it in a manner that showed she expected him to take it manfully. And he did. I was proud of my son."[1]

My mother and brother returned home—Joe had left for basic training in California by then—and my father prepared for the series of ten deep x-ray treatments that now were his only hope. He wrote to his four sisters and brother to tell them that he probably had less than a year to live, and two days later, began the deep x-ray treatments. Although his spirits were buoyed by going to daily Mass, hours spent at the Rochester library, emotional visits by his brother and sisters and neighbors, and the solicitous attention of my mother's sister Catherine, a nurse at St. Mary's Hospital, he soon felt the x-ray treatment's enervating effects. They caused fatigue and loss of appetite, and about halfway through them, he resisted the temptation to quit his treatment and return home.

But it was another kind of temptation that he was confronted with that he described in his diary. The night before my mother arrived to take him home after his final treatment, he returned to his hotel room and "was startled to find a woman sitting on my bed. She was beautiful, and dressed in a red velvet dressing gown. I stepped back out of the room because I thought I'd gotten into the wrong room. But I looked at the number and it was my room. The woman, a tall brunette, motioned me in. I recognized her as a fellow patient. I had seen her several times waiting for her x-ray treatments and had been struck by her beauty and exquisite clothes. The woman beckoned to me and I went. It was a scene about which I had tried to write, which in my wilder moments I might have even entertained, but a scene in which I, now fifty-five, felt abashed and ignorant. I suddenly felt bewildered. I know what she wanted me to do, but there I sat, like a bump on a log, and I had neither the strength nor the desire to carry the situation to its natural consequence. She cried bitterly and talked incessantly.

"She told me she had cancer of the throat and had less than a month to live. She was frightened and lonely, she said, and had watched me as I waited and felt that she wanted to possess me, perhaps the last man she would possess. I listened to her absolutely unmoved. I didn't have the least flicker of interest or curiosity about her. Suddenly I got up and told her very gently and without feeling any pity for her or myself, to go. She left the room with her beautiful head bent forward. On the bed she left the sash to her dressing gown. I wondered if she had done that deliberately and would be back after it. Then I took it and threw it out in the hall. I thought she would see it and think she had dropped it herself. The experience shook me, and I walked over to the bed and fall on my face and cried. I could still feel the warmth and the fragrance of her body on the bedspread."[2]

The next morning he had his final x-ray treatment and was formally dismissed. When my mother picked him up, they went back to the hotel a final night, and she smelled the woman's perfume, but my father couldn't because he had lost the sense of smell. "Somebody's been in here with some gorgeous smelling perfume," she said. Then, as they were leaving, the woman passed them in the hall and my mother recognized the woman's perfume. She turned to him and said, "Those bitches won't even let a man alone when he's sick and can't protect himself." That night, he went to sleep "wondering how she knew so much about such things. I made sure that my door was locked, and dreamed about our little silver-haired, blue-eyed daughter who had died on Christmas Eve some eighteen years ago. I would soon be joining her, I hoped."

After returning home, he was able to get dressed and walk around but his condition continued to worsen. And while he contributed to his "Post Chaise" and their "Countryside" columns and completed two short stories he had conceived during his stay in Rochester—one was called "The Temptation" and was based on his encounter with the woman in red —he temporarily discontinued his diary because of extreme fatigue and weakness. He also gave into my mother's urging him to receive the sacrament of Extreme Unction. As he wrote when he resumed his diary in early November, "Both Susan and Father Satory realized more than I did just what graces would accrue to me in the reception of this great sacrament. I have received five of the [seven] sacraments but this one frightened me. I knew I was going to die and very soon, but when I thought of the sacrament of the dying, I wanted to put it off. I kept saying I'm not that sick, and because I wasn't a bed patient yet, I felt it was incongruous."

But he received the sacrament one morning in mid-September after we took him to Mass. "I tried to kneel while Father Satory anointed me and said the age-old words of Holy Mother Church over her children who are in danger of death. The beautiful Latin words, the motions made by the priest, the smell of the sacramentals, my wife and boys kneeling beside me, suddenly overwhelmed me. I cried like a baby. But soon I recovered my composure and was led out of the church by my boys, who supported me on either side. . . . I felt as though something more than anointing me for death resulted from receiving Extreme Unction. It showered me with extraordinary grace. I cannot explain it in words but now I felt calm and at peace, physically, mentally, and above all spiritually. It came over me like a blinding flash just how important is a priest, one's own parish priest. . . . And it was then that I learned for the first time how rich is the Catholic Church. Most of my stories, I believe all of them, were set against the background of the Church, and my mind and heart were full of unwritten ones. But someone else would have to write them."

He continued to weaken, and by October, had lost the use of his left arm, and was mostly bed-ridden, "I knew that I would never use a typewriter again. The day it happened, I had typed furiously on a story, 'The Perfect Visit,' a silly thing, but it was the last story we typed. And it was about then that I developed a terrible cough. It would almost tear my throat out. Sometimes, a glass of hot milk would stay it, but every morning I dreaded to get up, even to urinate, because of that terrible spasm of coughing." And when my brother Joe came home on furlough, he stared at my father as he would stare at a stranger. "But it was good to have him home again. He had changed, too, but only in the way young men change, for the better," my father wrote.

About the same time, Claude Swanson, the editor of the *Fairmont Sentinel*, asked my mother if he could publish the very personal letter she had written him in September in response to his inquiry about my father. She had disclosed his cancer diagnosis and dire condition, which few people knew about, and told Swanson of my father's stoic reaction." Even though she had written "not for publication" on it, Swanson said the letter deserved to be read and it was her duty to let him publish it. She gave in, despite her second thoughts about doing so, and the letter created a sensation. It was reprinted in the Minneapolis newspaper and others around the U.S. and in several foreign countries as well, and it generated hundreds of letters. "Most of them were sympathetic, understanding ones that showed me so plainly what I had always known, the innate goodness of individuals," my father wrote.

By the end of October, when my father resumed his diary, he was shuttling back and forth between home, where my mother had installed a hospital bed which he at first refused to use, and the Blue Earth hospital. He received blood transfusions and was able to sleep with the aid of pills, but was racked with coughing spells, which sent pain through the affected kidney. Quarts of bloody fluid were drained from his stomach, and he was wracked by thirst. When his barber came to the house to shave him, he said the iron from the blood transfusions were making my father whiskers hard to shave. He could no longer remember what day it was, and could only say the rosary with his right hand. He made the last entry in his diary after he had been transferred a final time by ambulance to the local hospital "I feel like I am going on a long journey. It is like I am in two places. My thin body and swollen legs and parched lips are like parts of a cocoon that has been shed. I'm almost through with them. The hereafter is more real to me now than the here. I am almost anxious to be on my way. . . . Eventually I know I'll be reunited with my little daughter and my two sons who have preceded me. Susan will be left with our three sons. The family will be divided in half."

After he asked my mother to finish his diary as he dictated to her, she recounted a "strange experience," an overpowering stench that kept up for ten days until she asked God to give her strength after my father died, and "suddenly, the horrible stench was gone," and she realized that it was "a time of great joy and anticipation, and that my father was "ready for his eternal reward. I was privileged to catch the beauty of the glorious mysteries of the rosary, instead of dwelling too long in the sorrowful ones. We had already lived the sorrowful ones in our struggle for recognition in our writing. The joyful ones we had lived in our children." As she wrote of his final days, "He kept saying 'three in a hill.' I don't know what he meant by that. He said it was an old saying about planting. He wanted me to put it down. And he talked a great deal about heaven. I noticed several times during those last few days that he seemed to be turning his back on earthly things. It was as if he was impatient with us and anxious to be rid of the impedimentia of life itself."

On November 11, my father, feverish but apparently without much pain, reminded my mother that the 15th of November was his patron saint's day and said maybe he would die on St. Albert's Day. He said he wanted an autopsy performed although he was originally against it. The day before he died on November 14, she wrote that he was "reading a book in which he found a passage that bears particular interest to this story. He had marked it and wanted me to see it. The passage referred to the first indications of cancer in a person. It was contained in an obscure part of a book on the advancement of medical sciences and had been written by a Yale scientist about cancer. In it, he spoke of the depression that is often the first indication of cancer. And Albert said, 'Susan, here is how I felt last March when you were at your brother's funeral in Tennessee. It came over me suddenly, this awful desolation. I lost the will to live. Now I know what it was. I think cancer is some kind of a virus and it took hold of me and caused me to feel so depressed.'"

On the morning he died, Father Satory brought Holy Communion, and said it was probably the last time he would receive it. Then he urged my mother to write his column, as she had done for several weeks, to meet his deadline. She went to the hospital office while a neighbor stayed with him. "My mind was a blank, and I don't know what I wrote. I asked God

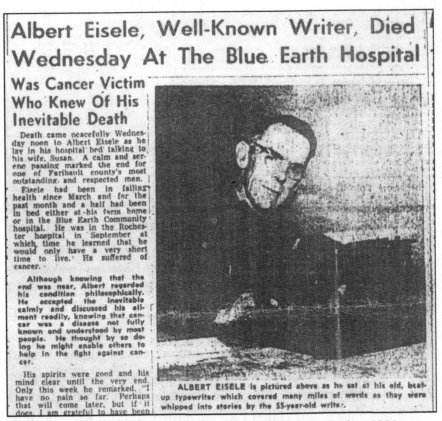

Albert Eisele, Well-Known Writer, Died Wednesday At The Blue Earth Hospital

Was Cancer Victim Who Knew Of His Inevitable Death

Death came peacefully Wednesday noon to Albert Eisele as he lay in his hospital bed talking to his wife, Susan. A calm and serene passing marked the end for one of Faribault county's most outstanding and respected men.

Eisele had been in failing health since March and for the past month and a half had been in bed either at his farm home or in the Blue Earth Community hospital. He was in the Rochester hospital in September at which time he learned that he would only have a very short time to live. He suffered of cancer.

Although knowing that the end was near, Albert regarded his condition philosophically. He accepted the inevitable calmly and discussed his ailment readily, knowing that cancer was a disease not fully known and understood by most people. He thought by so doing he might enable others to help in the fight against cancer.

His spirits were good and his mind clear until the very end. Only this week he remarked, "I have no pain so far. Perhaps that will come later, but if it does, I am grateful to have been

ALBERT EISELE is pictured above as he sat at his old, beat-up typewriter which covered many miles of words as they were whipped into stories by the 55-year-old writer.

Albert's death reported in the Blue Earth newspaper, November 1951.

95

WEEK OF DECEMBER 3, 1951

Countryside

By Albert and Susan Boele

As most of you know by now, Albert died on November 14, after an illness of some few months with cancer. He was well-prepared and in no great pain, conscious, and able to write or dictate until the end.

✧

For us the experience has been a wonderful one in every way. God has been very good to us to give Albert to us as a husband and father, and his death has brought us close to the eternal values. The boys and I hope to live as bravely as he has died, and some day to be reunited with him in heaven.

✧

pensated by the knowledge that their beloved one has reached the goal for which he was born and for which he has striven during his life time.

✧

And our life in its sorrow has suddenly become glorious.

This experience should serve as a lesson to our readers. Don't live in the future. Maybe there won't be a tomorrow. If you want to take a trip, take it. Lay off some of that hard work and worry. Spend more time with each other. Don't let the material things of life swallow you up to the extent that you forget the sweet, meaningful things of the soul and the mind.

Susan tells readers of "Countryside" column about Albert's death.

to help me. It came out in chunks. I told his readers what he has asked me to do and that I had tried to do it. It just took a few minutes. I ended it with these words: 'So now I have written this week's 'Post Chaise,' a page short because the going's tough, and I can go back up to Albert's room and tell him I did it. And he'll feel better. Keep on praying for us." Then I went back to his room, bent over him and said, 'Albert, I wrote your 'Post Chaise.' He opened his eyes, smiled, raised his right hand as if to bless me, and said weakly, 'Good.' Then he said it again more weakly, and was gone." No struggle. No nothing. I raced to the telephone and called Father Satory and he was there in no time. Our family doctor, George Drexler, pronounced him dead. Father Satory said a few prayers, held Albert's hand and said, 'Albert, pray for me.' I bent over and kissed his calm, beautiful face and left the room. Then I called the boys and told them."

When she told readers of the "Countryside" column of his death, she said he "was well-prepared and in no great pain, conscious and able to write or dictate until the end." Despite her sorrow, she said "the experience has been wonderful in every way. God has very good to us as to give Albert as a husband and father, and his death has brought us close to the eternal values. The boys and I hope to live as bravely as he has died, and some day to be reunited with him in heaven." She said he "asked me to personally thank you for the things you have done for him," and added, "If ever a man got his flowers while he was living, after a life of comparative obscurity and literary toiling in the dark and almost alone, he did. His short stories will live because they are made of immortal stuff." She noted that he had written two stories after he was no longer able to type and they were immediately accepted, and one was published a day after his death. She ended by citing my father's firm belief in the power of the written word, and saying, "I hope God puts a pencil in his hand first thing."

Note

[1]He took hundreds of notes during his stay at the Mayo Clinic, continuing a lifetime habit. For example, "Wait for doctor in Mayo Clinic office. Ceiling ten feet up, oak panels halfway. Like confessional. I wait for doctor, but priest waits for sinner." And. "Lame man lighting cigarette beside pillar; frailty of man compared with sturdy pillar." And the many Negro patients: "No Jim Crow in Rochester.

Chapter Eight

Out of the Humdrum

MY MOTHER LIVED ALMOST a third of a century after my father died, and never remarried. But she filled her remaining thirty-two years with much living. She continued to write her weekly "Penny Pencil" and "Countryside" columns while contributing monthly columns for *The Witness* magazine and *Columbia*, the national Knights of Columbus magazine, in collaboration with Florence Hynes Willette. She was also a correspondent for several regional newspapers and radio stations and was usually lugging a heavy 4x5 Speed Graphic camera; was active in civic and professional organizations, received many writing and civic awards and was a doting grandmother of eight.

However, her transition to widowhood wasn't easy, as I discovered from a letter she sent in December 1951, shortly after my father died, to my brother Joe, who was in the Army in California (he was hoping for a hardship discharge, which he got in early 1952 and returned to operate the farm). In the three-page single-spaced typewritten letter, she said she spent $500 on funeral expenses "and have almost that much yet to pay. Counting the $1,300 we owe at the bank we owe close to $4,500 around

Susan as most people saw her when she reported the news.

town and I have exactly $400 in the bank. What will happen I don't know. We had the estate probated and I was at the lawyer's office today and had to post a $2,000 bond myself."

She went on to say she couldn't sell the farm because it was tied up in the estate, but added: "If worst comes to worst, I can have a sale and sell the livestock and machinery , but they say second-hand machinery is not selling and I would hate to do that unless it had to be done—and stay here and rent out the land. . . . We owe so much money around town that we will have to be very discreet in what we do, because I am a widow now and a woman is at a disadvantage over a man. As long as Dad was alive it was different. And none of us has a right to

99

Week of July 8, 1957.

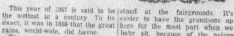

Countryside

— by —

SUSAN FRAWLEY EISELE

This year of 1957 is said to be the wettest in a century. To be exact, it was in 1858 that the great rains, world-wide, did havoc.

The newspapers in this country, in Europe and in Asia commented on the swollen rivers, inundated plains, impassable roads and the lack of sunshine.

"Well, it has cleared up for another shower," became the standing remark.

✦ ✦ ✦

Here in our county the spring was late and stormy and the rains incessant. Only the highest ground could be planted and seed rotted in the ground. Creeks became rivers, roads mired down into fathomless mud and bottom lands took on the appearance of permanent lakes. Still it continued to rain. This went on until into July, when it cleared up and the rest of the year was a normal one. But crop damage had been great and the harvest was small.

✦ ✦ ✦

A similar pattern followed in 1859, but less widespread, and not as devastating. Two late, wet springs and long, cold characterized the years of 1858-59. Then the weather righted itself and fabulous crops were grown.

✦ ✦ ✦

Several times this year we have taken the car and on impulse driven out of town into the country, to a roadside park, say, on the river bank, to the farm, over a remote road built on peat beds, through the old lake bed country, across the still virgin stretches of prairie land, in any direction. The longest of these spur-of-the-moment drives have not been more than ten miles in length. Often only half that long.

But each time we have been fortunate enough to come on some enchanting sight. It may have been coincidence. Or it might be some small, sweet, celestial tinkling. This sudden urge must come from somewhere and from someone.

✦ ✦ ✦

When Albert was living, he always called us out to see or to hear or to smell or to feel the beauty and the wonder of nature's unfoldings. Maybe he still does. All we know is that we seem to be in the right place at the right time.

For example, early this week we drove out to the farm to baby sit for a few hours while Rose did her stint at the church food

stand at the fairgrounds. It's easier to have the grandsons up here for the most part when we baby sit, because of the nature of our work. But this time we decided to go out there. We took a south road instead of the one we usually take. Joe's field of flax was in bloom. To come on your first field of flax in bloom each season, is to feel your spirit being crushed in a press, like grapes are pressed for wine. It was at its precise and ultimate moment of glory waiting for us.

✦ ✦ ✦

Later this week on our way to Fairmont, we drove, again by impulse, over a mile of little traveled road west of East Chain. Lush, waist-high, ripening grasses rippled like the sea, and made the same sipping sound. Here we found our first milkweed of the year, a colony of it in bloom.

The fencelands and the brush were alive with birds, blue birds, red birds, yellow birds, striped birds and mottled birds. Something had brought them there to congregate. Maybe it was the milkweed in bloom, or perhaps they found a wild raspberry patch. They paid not the slightest notice to our car passing. We drove slowly to watch them more closely. We have never seen so many different kinds of brightly-colored birds assembled together before.

✦ ✦ ✦

Does anyone have a recipe for 'second day cake? We have it somewhere, but can't find it. It has appeared in this column. The cake was served traditionally on the next day after the wedding. A bride-to-be has asked for the recipe. Please send to Susan Frawley Eisele, Blue Earth, Minnesota, Box 365.

✦ ✦ ✦

One young girl we know has gone to Omaha for a vacation. She told us that she had made enough to take the trip by baby sitting. "And I'm going to baby sit while I'm there, too!" she added.

✦ ✦ ✦

We were at a surprise party not long ago, where the guests did up the dishes afterwards. All of us helped, except one guest. Her mother said, "She is studying for her master's degree, and she shouldn't have to put her hands in a dishpan, do you think?"

Susan's July 8, 1957, "Countryside" column.

spend money we don't have as long as we have creditors who have to wait for their money. And I hope to get out from under that as soon as I can, but it won't be quick and it won't be easy. But I am not going to run away from it, I don't scare easily, and with the help of God, we'll weather whatever comes." At the same time, she made it clear she would continue her writing. "I hope to keep up Albert's Post Chaise column for the time being as I can use the money. I was in Minneapolis last week and left Albert's journal on his illness with the editor of the *Star Journal* as he was interested in seeing what could be done with it. I saw the Midland Cooperative

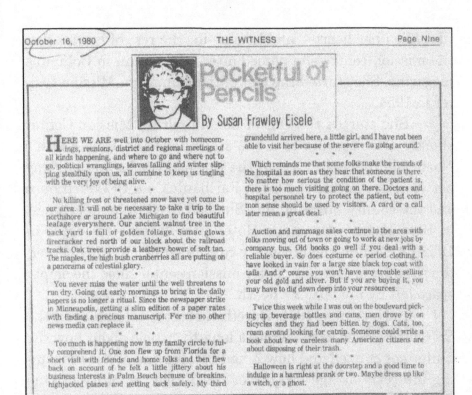

Pocketful of Pencils
By Susan Frawley Eisele

HERE WE ARE well into October with homecomings, reunions, district and regional meetings of all kinds happening, and where to go and where not to go, political wranglings, leaves falling and winter slipping stealthily upon us, all combine to keep us tingling with the very joy of being alive.

*   *   *

No killing frost or threatened snow have yet come in our area. It will not be necessary to take a trip to the northshore or around Lake Michigan to find beautiful leafage everywhere. Our ancient walnut tree in the back yard is full of golden foliage. Sumac glows firecracker red north of our block about the railroad tracks. Oak trees provide a leathery bower of soft tan. The maples, the high bush cranberries all are putting on a panorama of celestial glory.

*   *   *

You never miss the water until the well threatens to run dry. Going out early mornings to bring in the daily papers is no longer a ritual. Since the newspaper strike in Minneapolis, getting a slim edition of a paper rates with finding a precious manuscript. For me no other news media can replace it.

*   *   *

Too much is happening now in my family circle to fully comprehend it. One son flew up from Florida for a short visit with friends and home folks and then flew back on account of he felt a little jittery about his business interests in Palm Beach because of breakins, highjacked planes and getting back safely. My third grandchild arrived here, a little girl, and I have not been able to visit her because of the severe flu going around.

Which reminds me that some folks make the rounds of the hospital as soon as they hear that someone is there. No matter how serious the condition of the patient is, there is too much visiting going on there. Doctors and hospital personnel try to protect the patient, but common sense should be used by visitors. A card or a call later mean a great deal.

*   *   *

Auction and rummage sales continue in the area with folks moving out of town or going to work at new jobs by company bus. Old books go well if you deal with a reliable buyer. So does costume or period clothing. I have looked in vain for a large size black top coat with tails. And o° course you won't have any trouble selling your old gold and silver. But if you are buying it, you may have to dig down deep into your resources.

*   *   *

Twice this week while I was out on the boulevard picking up beverage bottles and cans, men drove by on bicycles and they had been bitten by dogs. Cats, too, roam around looking for catnip. Someone could write a book about how careless many American citizens are about disposing of their trash.

*   *   *

Halloween is right at the doorstep and a good time to indulge in a harmless prank or two. Maybe dress up like a witch, or a ghost.

people and they are going to use the Countryside column every week instead of two, so that will help."

Finally, she told Joe she didn't miss Albert "like I thought Iwould—God has been very good to us. I feel his nearness and that he is watching over us and I am here alone a lot of the time and feel perfectly contented. I want to keep on living and doing in such a way as to keep faith with him and do my dead level best to keep things going here."

She eventually was able to pay her debts after Joe returned to run the farm, and she moved to an apartment in a Blue Earth hotel as Arnold went off to college and I finished high school. But her most ambitious undertaking, and the one

that filled her heart— and house—for the rest of her life was
the mission center she named after her column in Columbia
magazine. She started the Out of the Humdrum Mission Center in 1954.

She started the Out of the Humdrum Mission Center
shortly after moving to a two-story house on Blue Earth's
North Main Street, next to the railroad tracks and halfway
between the gothic red brick Faribault County Courthouse
and the county fairgrounds. (She had lived in an apartment
in Blue Earth's Constans Hotel after leaving the farm in
1952.) Although she obviously continued her writing career,
the Humdrum Mission Center mission center filled the empty
space left by my father's death.

In November 1962, Gareth Hiebert, a columnist for the
St. Paul Pioneer Press, wrote a lengthy article about how the
center got started and how it had become one of her consuming interests at age sixty-five. Headlined "A Story of One
Woman's Attack on Need: Gifts From All U.S. Flood Blue
Earth Home," he said it was "an innocuous little paragraph
[in her *Columbia* magazine column] that planted the seed of
her unusual philanthropy." She told him a student at the
Saint Paul Seminary "wrote and asked whether I could mention that he would like to have some broken rosaries."[1] She
did, and broken and unbroken rosaries began arriving by the
gross, along with other religious articles, clothing, bedding,
games, jewelry, and other items. "Like Topsy, Susan's mission
growed and growed and growed, and now, eighty to ninety
packages arrive at 631 N. Main Street every week," Hiebert
wrote. "A few weeks ago, a woman in Brockton, Mass., sent
1,800 pounds of old clothing and new apparel that cost her
$133 in postage. With much of it comes comes letters, each

reciting a chapter of human drama. Finery designed for weddings that never took place. Bathrobes and slippers never worn by persons who had died. One woman sent a complete assortment of baby clothes and this note: 'These were given me at baby showers. My baby was dead at birth. God bless the little girl or boy who can use these.'

"To get the true perspective of Susan Eisele's mission is to understand that its operation is superimposed as a labor of love on a daily regimen that would fatigue a woman forty years her junior. Long before dawn, the lights in the house next to the railroad tracks have been burning. Between getting breakfast for herself and a big, brick-shade cat named Rusty, Susan has been phoning the sheriff and police chief for any overnight violence. By 8:00 a.m., she has called the funeral homes for deaths, checked out details of last night's city council meeting, and taken three items about club meetings. All these she sets down on a typewriter, perched on the somewhat cluttered desk. Some of this news will be sent to the *Fairmont Sentinel* before 9:00 a.m. or given to an announcer for a Fairmont radio station who broadcasts her daily newscast at 11:00 a.m. from the Constans Hotel. 'I used to broadcast it myself when I lived at the hotel, but I don't think women's voices sound good on the radio, so I just write the script. Except sometimes I'll do interviews.'"

Although she sent the stuff out as fast as it came in—a trucking company hauled thousands of pounds without charge and church and welfare agencies made their own pickups—she relied on contributions and her own funds to finance the mission center, but didn't like to admit that she often goes without a meal or skimps on groceries to buy postage. She said she would not turn anyone down who needed something. "There would be no distinction as far as religion and color was concerned. I may be a Catholic but I grew up in Tennessee as the only non-Protestant in town. I think that charity is one level where we can demonstrate the brotherhood of man."

Hiebert wrote that every Saturday morning, she "says a little prayer" and begins writing whatever comes to mind for her weekly "Countryside" column, which was syndicated to some two dozen newspapers in Minnesota, Iowa, and South Dakota, as well as her other columns. "Maybe I'll write about the weather, birds, Rusty, a recipe for pork shanks or something my five grandchildren said or did." She described her columns as "a farm-sized helping of the little things about country living that stir sentiment among city folks," before spending the rest of her week on her mission work. "My mission project is the biggest thing in my life now. Sometimes, as I sift through the boxes, I realize the tremendous charity and generosity that abounds in the world. There is something almost sanctifying about being able to channel this generosity into places where it will do good."

In another column in 1968, she wrote, "No matter how much comes in, it is just a drop in the bucket and we again ask you to share with us any bedding and heavy clothing. It doesn't have to be new or in perfect condition. We have calls, too, for yarn, cotton and woolen material that can be made into quilts or comforters and clothing." She gave her address as usual and added, "If we aren't home when you come, please leave your boxes in the garage, on the front porch or the side porch."

And in a 1973 column, she declared that her mission center "isn't just a place to dump old clothes and such. To it comes drama, comedy, and tragedy, patrons of romance unfulfilled as well as stories of personal struggles almost unbelievable. A novel could be written about a mission center, but not by the person manning it—he or she is too busy and too concerned about trying to fill a few of the immediate needs of those who cannot or will not help themselves. Trends in fashion and way of life could be foretold at a mission center by the kinds of things being discarded. Economic values could be judged. Preferences in books and hobbies and handicrafts show up here first. Actually, each box of mission material that comes could tell an interesting story, if one had time to listen. . . . Coming this morning with some religious articles were two strings of voodoo beads, the first I had ever seen. The are weird looking. So you see, a mission center is not a dull place at all. I don't feel that I am wasting my time, because it is giving me more than I can give it."

She begged readers for contributions of clothing, household goods, books, games, jewelry, and anything else they wanted to get rid of. "We are in need of soap, heavy underwear or other suitable winter clothing, bedding, and baby clothes," she wrote in 1975. "If you have anything to share, please send or bring it here. We never should have started this project. The only reason we did was a selfish one. We weren't doing it for love of God or man, but just to see if anyone was reading the column. We thought it would peter out. But instead it has grown into an almost full-time project. And it has become the greatest joy of my life."

The voluminous files I inherited from my bothers included hundreds of the columns she wrote until entering an assisted living home in 1982, two years before her death. In addition to all of my father's writings, the files included countless letters she wrote to me while I was in college, in the Army, playing professional baseball in the Cleveland Indians farm system, working as a reporter in Mankato, St. Paul, and Washington, and as Vice-President Mondale's press secretary from 1977 to 1981. Often, she wrote on the back of the proofs or typewritten copies of her columns, usually in longhand but sometimes typewritten, some as long or longer than her columns. And she sent me dozens of articles about her or family and friends.

Her letters were filled with personal observations and comments. For example, in January 1957, she wrote, "I'm still fighting television. I don't want to get involved, I say in protest. I rebel against having to sit, slave-like, in its compelling and overpowering presence, and besides, I haven't time. My life is already too complicated. But a portable TV, now, well, maybe that would be different," while writing about becoming attached to Arnie's portable radio.

She loved being a grandmother and reading to her grandchildren. "We laugh and clown and hug and kiss and sometimes there are tears and catastrophes, but how can we measure the complete joy of grandmotherhood?" she wrote in July 1957. "They say our society is a classless one. Don't be silly. Being a grandmother automatically places you in a special aristocracy."

And she often wrote about her Persian cat Rusty. When she told readers of her *Witness* column in 1961 that he ate corn on the cob, the *Des Moines Register* picked up the story, and it went all over the world. But she refused requests for photos, explaining that they could easily be faked. And in another 1961 column, she said Rusty was "developing an embarrassing habit. Whenever anyone comes, he stands between us, sniffs the visitor and makes a swift appraisal. If it is someone who does not like cats, he whines and fusses. But if the visitor is to his liking, he gets too friendly. After they leave, he settles down and begins purring, as much as to say he could do without company. A cat at times is a jealous taskmaster." And when a neighbor's dog charmed her in 1962, she wrote, "I have a cat that is aloof, unpredictable and downright nasty to folks who come here. I have to cater to his whims and wonder if will go back to where he came from [but] he is beautiful and he is jealous and he likes me. But he better watch his step. That good old collie made a fine impression on me." Finally, in 1971, she reported that the sixteen-year-old cat died. "Joe came in from the farm, and we buried him in the back yard under the old walnut tree."

And in 1972, she advised young people who aspired to be writers, "Unless you get a break, you have to start from the bottom. You won't become an editor or a commentator or a script writer overnight. If I were to live my life over, I'd just get some sharp pencils, some notebooks, a dictionary, and go out into the highways and byways and dig out a story. I'd read everything I could get hands on. I'd listen and look and think and brush shoulders with the whole world. Then I'd go into some newspaper office, radio station, or television studio and try to see the top man.

If you land a job, great. You might have to do obituaries for a start. All right, practice on them, make them interesting. Spell the names correctly. Poke around in all the departments if you can. Don't be tied to one segment of writing. Try them all. You'll make it some way. You may not get rich. You probably won't. But you will call your soul your own and as long as a man does that, he is the master of his own destiny."

Because she lived next to railroad tracks, hoboes often appeared at her door asking for food or clothing. She regularly wrote about them, and often attended an annual hobo festival in Britt, Iowa. Her favorite, a frequent visitor whom she called "my boyfriend," was Richard Wilson, aka "the Pennsylvania Kid," who was crowned national hobo king four times. She even displayed his photo above her typewriter desk. When asked if she was afraid of hoboes, she replied, "No, I am not. Hoboes are not criminals. They could be called the nation's first dissenters, breaking out of the establishment in a peaceful way, and living their lives as they choose. I kind of admire them. Next week, I'll give you the recipe for Mulligan Stew, which I have used many times. This recipe is the one they will be using in Britt, Iowa, at this year's Hobo Day."

Another favorite subject in all her writings was the surrounding landscape, and its inhabitants. "Now is a perfect time to take a drive along some country road and look at the roadside growth," she wrote in 1972. "I found such a stretch recently straddling the Iowa-Minnesota state line. The grasses were so tall and heavy and so thick that they looked matted. And as the wind blew, they undulated, like waves on a lake. The illusion was so striking that I could have been driving through water-filled ditches. Nature is so lavish." In the same column, she wrote of seeing a toad, a bumblebee, a butterfly, an owl and a garter snake. Another visitor here is a large blue-jay, a killer at heart. He has taken possession of the bird feeders and pecks at all birds approaching. The baby birds in the neighborhood are so frightened with him around that they sit on the ground and cry, shivering in fright."

She also still missed my father after nearly a quarter century. "Today is the 24th anniversary of Albert's death," she wrote in November 1975. "It sometimes seems like it happened yesterday. Then again, I think it was a dream and didn't happen. Death will forever be an enigma. He seems so near to me and I still forget that he is dead. If I come on a news story or an incident that I think would interest him, I say, 'Albert,' and then catch myself."

Susan meets a fellow Southerner at the White House, 1977.

A few months earlier, *Minneapolis Tribune* columnist George Peterson noted that my mother had limited her column writing at age seventy-eight to devote herself to her mission center. "There are days when I can't sit still because there is so much to do and see," she told him. "So I thank God. He has let me live so long and given me the opportunity of learning more about His wonderful universe." She always felt that the world was brought to her doorstep through her writing, as she wrote in one of her last columns. "I'm no traveler so I sit here and meet the world the lazy way. Kings and queens, dreamers, travelers, inventors, scientists, the high and lowly—and then I do the dishes and tackle the dandelions."

In August 1978, the world literally came to her as Vice-President Mondale—I accompanied him—flew over Blue Earth in an Air Force helicopter to be honored by his hometown of Elmore. My mother was present and of course met Mondale. A week later, U.S. Secretary of Transportation Brock Adams came to Blue Earth to officiate as a golden spike was driven at a rest stop just north of town to mark the completion of the I-90 Interstate Highway, which cut across southern Minnesota and linked Seattle with Boston.[2] My mother later told me she was glad that Mondale didn't attend because it would "politicize" the event. But she also said Adams was "a rather dull speaker."

But the thrill of her life came on her eightieth birthday in 1977 when she came to Washington to visit me and my wife and two children. I took her to my office and Mondale greeted her in his office in the White House. After a few minutes, he said "Susan, there's somebody else here I'd like you to meet. His name is Jimmy." He took her into the Oval Office and introduced her to President Carter as "one of the best Democrats in Minnesota." Carter greeted his fellow Southerner with a hug and kiss, and posed for photographs with his arm around her. "I just about fell over,' she recalled. "I went up to him, and we hugged and kissed each other, just automatically. He's older looking than he shows and he's shorter. But he's so outgoing and so warm that you just love him." And naturally, the photographs and article about the meeting generated a host of "Susan Meets the President" headlines in Minnesota and around the country.[3]

As she grew older, my mother often wondered out loud whether she could continue writing and running her mission center. "I don't know how much longer I am going to be able to keep up my column writing," she wrote in her "Country-side" column as the new year began in 1974. "I still love doing it, and suppose I'll be keeping at it until I get senile. But the mission work, which I love too, continues to grow to the point where I am going to have to make a decision."[4] And when she turned seventy-eight in 1975, she wrote, "There are days when I don't feel like working or even thinking, but I know that comes with age. Then there are days, most of them, when I can't sit still because there is so much to do and see. So I thank God that He has let me live this long and has given me the opportunity of learning more about His wonderful universe. I can't understand those persons who won't tell their age or grieve about getting old."

But she was clearly showing signs of aging. In 1978, she was having trouble walking and keeping her balance, and she told me she was not feeling well and was losing weight for no apparent reason. Her doctor urged her to have someone stay with her at night, which grandchildren and neighbors did. She was soon forced to give up most of her writing and mission center work, and in 1981, entered St. Luke's Nursing Home, where she was joined by her thrice-widowed sister Catharine. In March 1982, she received an outpouring of love and support from the community when the mayor of Blue Earth proclaimed "Susan Frawley Eisele Day." The local newspaper published a two-page "To Susan, With Love!" special section that included photos of her with her family at St. Luke's and some forty letters from people ranging from Presidents Reagan and Carter to a grandson who said her response when learning of the special day asked, "Why didn't they honor someone who was working?"

Notes

[1] It was probably my brother Arnold, then studying for the priesthood.

[2] A sixty-foot statue of the Jolly Green Giant, symbol of the company that operated a packing plant in Blue Earth, also made its debut, overlookeing the rest stop, but some people noted that the Pillsbury Company had just bought the Green Giant Company and joked that the Pillsbury Doughboy would soon replace the Jolly Green Giant. But it remains to this day one of the city's top tourist attractions. Unfortunately, Blue Earth's mayor died of a heart attack the day before the dedication.

[3] Ironically, the story of her meeting with Carter and two accompanying photos appeared on the front page of the *Mankato Free Press* on June 11, 1977, just above a story about Martin Luther King's confessed killer, James Earl Ray, escaping from a prison near Knoxville, Tennessee, not far from her hometown of Newport. He was later captured and returned to prison, where he died in 1998.

[4] She was also convinced her phone was being bugged by Republicans looking for damaging information about Carter and Mondale, and complained to the president of the telephone company, a prominent Republican, who dismissed her concern.

Epilogue

Susan and Albert

THE LAST TIME I SAW my mother was a few months before her death. When I told her I intended to speak at her funeral, she admonished me not to brag on her. But I did anyway. She died on April 4, 1984, and a large crowd turned out for her funeral at SS. Peter and Paul's Catholic Church. In my eulogy, I cited her often-expressed wish that "heaven is as exciting as life on earth," I said I was sure it was, and that she probably had "already asked God at least six times, 'What's new?'" And considering her lifelong interest in helping the poor, I also said I wouldn't be surprised if she'd already opened 'Susan's Celestial Mission Center.'"

I noted that she was a loyal Democrat all her life who was actively involved in the party and intensely interested in the political process. And with her good sense of humor, she would have appreciated the irony of being buried by a Republican undertaker. I said she was "a writer's writer," and quoted one of her admirers, who said "The thread of middle American values runs through all of her writing. It reflects home, family, church, the land and the democratic process. . . . She's American Gothic, 1980s style."

After going back and reading some of her vast output over the years in her newspaper and magazine columns, and her correspondence with family and friends, I cited several qualities I thought summed her up and which she'd like to be remembered by. "First of all, she had an intense, passion, consuming and insatiable curiosity about people and the life around her. She wrote about everything and everybody because her interests were universal. For example, she once wrote about misplacing her upper teeth. 'I said to myself. That's silly, who cares what happens to Mrs. Eisele's teeth? My head said leave it out and my heart said put it in. My heart won. Ever since, folks have been stopping me on the street and writing me, telling me how glad they were when they read it. Consensus was that it happens to so many folks, but all of them think it just happens to them. Which goes to show you that a writer is a gambler. You just don't know what readers will react to—and that is what makes the game interesting.'"

Second, I said she had "wonderful powers of observation and a descriptive ability that enabled her to transform the most ordinary and mundane things into objects of almost Byzantine splendor. She had a gift of being able to discover universal values in the particular, values that everyone recognized immediately once they were pointed out." And I cited two of her columns. In May 1972, she wrote, "Lady bugs and box elder bugs made their appearance this week. Dandelions are up and I hoed some of them out, feeling pious and as dedicated as an evangelist. Going after them will get harder as the season advances, and like sin, will be with us forever."

And in March 1975, she wrote, "As I grow older, I marvel more at the beauty and significance of life as viewed from a window or door in one's own home. I agree with Pascal that it would take a thousand years to record the simple, everyday doings that go on right before your eyes. You don't have to go out to see the world if you just let it come by to see you." I quoted the great Irish writer James Joyce's admonition to "Write what is in your heart, not what is in your head. As for me, if I can get to the heart of Dublin, I can get to the heart of any city in the world." And I said that was true of my mother's writing, "whether about the weather, children, animals, insects, weeds in her garden, or county fairs. All of which she wrote about frequently. She was truly able to get to the heart of this community and rural America."

A third quality was her tolerance for the great range of diversity in human behavior. "She was equally at home among all classes and ranks of people, and she welcomed and reveled in all kinds of life styles. The best example of this is the column she wrote in August 1970, after visiting my brother Arnold in Florida. For some reason, he took her to a night club to see some go-go dancers. She wrote matter-of-factly about the nudity she'd witnessed and how the exotic world of the dancers seems so far from reality. Then, during intermission, she was on the way to the restroom when she wandered into the dressing room and overheard two of the dancers. 'I heard one of the go-go girls saying that the man she was living with was not coming back, and that her mother was going to take her baby, and she was going to keep on working. She put her head in her hands and sobbed. I could have cried myself. My mind raced, and I tried to make sense out of all I had seen and heard at the night club. All that I could come up with was feeling that we are more or less all alike under the skin and the veneer. She was selling her body; I am selling my mind. Take your choice."

A fourth quality was her ability to transcend the barriers and speak to all age groups. Her writing was as relevant to her children and grandchildren's generation as to her own. Several years ago she wrote a letter to my daughter Kitty, who had just visited New York City for the first time, telling her in great detail about her own trip there in 1936 when she was named the nation's best rural columnist. And in another column, she wrote about walking along the railroad tracks near her house with her oldest grandson Matthew. "We found such interesting sights. Most exciting for me were the first wild roses of the season. Albert and I always competed with each other in sighting this beautiful flower's appearance. The clump that Matthew and I found is growing close to the tracks and is covered with bloom. Stop by and I'll show you where it is. It will do your soul good."

A fifth quality that was apparent in her writing was her sense of compassion. She had her share of sadness and tragedy but it never embittered her or made her less conscious of the suffering of the poor and the less fortunate. She loved her missions work and considered it second in importance only to her writing. In going through her writing, I discovered the column she wrote in 1937 when her own mother was dying. "What kind of column does one write as one's mother lies dying? Should there be rejoicing? Rejoicing that a noble soul is about to fulfill its destiny, a courageous life about to lock up its house and move into a new one. Do not lament, because a dying mother, could she speak, would smile and say, 'Go make yourself a cup of coffee, children, don't worry about me. This other thing can wait." Yes, death can wait. Patiently and complacently, and why not? Only life is impatient, impatient over little things, anxious for this day to be done, waiting for tomorrow—bread to bake, floors to be mopped, overalls to be mended. There is no time for dying."

A final quality of my mother's was her strong and unshakeable faith. "She was an active member of this parish and cared deeply about it and about her religious duties. She also believed in the promise of resurrection that we heard in today's Gospel. I think her faith is evident in the column she wrote after my father died in 1951. 'When he first knew that he was doomed, I thought to myself, this is the end of my world. I thought of death with an almost terror. Of the emptiness it would leave in me. But now I know that death is beautiful, that it is only the beginning, that those who are left behind are strengthened and compensated by the knowledge that their beloved one has reached the goal for which he was born and for which he has striven during his lifetime. And our life in its sorry has suddenly become glorious. This experience should serve as a lesson to all. Don't live in the future. Maybe there won't be a tomorrow. If you want to take a trip, take it. Lay off some of that hard work and worry. Spent more time with each other. Don't let the material things of life swallow you up to the extent that you forget the sweet, meaningful things of the soul and the mind.'"

Finally, she recalled the moment of my father's death in 1951. "The morning he died, he fussed because his own column in the Blue Earth paper wasn't written. To kind of soothe him, I went down to the hospital office and wrote it. Then I went back to his room and told him. He said, 'Good,' and was gone. I hope God puts a pencil in his hand first thing." I ended my eulogy by saying, "I hope God puts a pencil in my mother's hand first thing—and then proceeds to tell her all the news He knows."

As for my father, I can think of no better way of honoring him than by comparing two of his many short stories that illustrate the development of his writing style. The first was "The Brother Who Came," which appeared in *The Commonweal* in February 1939, and was called by David Marshall, a Fordham University professor, "one of the finest short stories ever written." The second was "The Short Day," published by *America* magazine in August 1951, three months before his death.

"The Brother Who Came" was included in *Our Father's House*, an anthology of Catholic writers compiled by Sister Mariella Gable, and was published by Sheed & Ward in 1945. She described him as "a farmer—just an average farmer, he insists, who rises early for milking and toils with plow and reaper through a fourteen-hour day on his farm near Blue Earth, Minnesota. Yet he finds time to be a poet, a short story writer, a novelist, a columnist, a husband, and the father of three sons. He contributes a weekly column to the *Blue Earth Post*, and he and his wife write a joint weekly column on farm life, which appears in twenty-five Iowa and Minnesota newspapers. His short stories have been published in *The Commonweal*, *The Catholic World*, *America*, and other magazines, and he was a regular contributor [of poems] to *Spirit*. His art is stark, stripped. What he has to say is truth seen so clearly that it surprises. He writes of the ancient verities. About them clings the odor of the soil." Sister Mariella considered his story as "peripheral fiction— that which does not have a Catholic message but is strong in the local color of Catholic faith. . . . Its theme is that those who have the least often give the most—as true for Protestants as for Catholics, and equally true for persons with no religion whatsoever."

But "The Short Day" written some twenty years later, displayed none of those faults, drawing an admiring note from Bruce Bliven, editorial director of *The New Republic*, who wrote, "That was a touching little sketch of yours in America for August 18, and beautifully done. My envious congratulations." The story takes place in 1946 as a raging snowstorm forces a country school to close early and Mr. Stagemann picks up his four children and brings them home. They share a snowed-in weekend at their farm, while enjoying sumptuous meals and snacks prepared by the German-born Mrs. Stagemann. The snow has prevented a weekend mail delivery to the farm but a neighbor drives to town and picks up his and the Stagemanns' mail, which includes the first letter in five years from Mrs. Stagemann's sister in Germany.

Urged by her husband and children to read the letter aloud in German, they make fun of the strange-sounding language. Then, as she translates it, it becomes clear that it is a plea for help. The sister and her family are starving in postwar Germany and she begs Mrs. Stagemann to send them food immediately. "Tonight I had to send Joseph and the children to bed without any supper," the sister writes, "and the worst of it is that there is nothing in the house for tomorrow morning. May God help us!" Mrs. Stagemann collapses in tears and her husband sternly sends the children to bed. But as they troop upstairs, one of them calls out, "Don't forget the buckwheat pancakes and the pork sausages tomorrow morning!" Stagemann tells his wife he didn't know of her family's plight and is sorry he made her read the letter. He promises to send food to the starving family the next day. But he couldn't comfort her, "and for a moment he wished that the storm were still raging, with the roar of the wind muffling the sound of her crying."

"The Brother Who Came" and "The Short Day" can serve as brackets for his nearly eighty short stories that appeared in Catholic and rural life magazines from 1937 until shortly after his death in 1951, along with more than a dozen poems, and of course, hundreds of newspaper columns as well. He also wrote some forty other short stories and a novel that were rejected, and almost seventy more stories and dozens of poems that remain unpublished.

Despite my father's vast literary output, it was exceeded by that of my mother, who wrote newspaper and magazine columns filled with personal commentary and observations for most of her eighty-six years. While almost impossible to quantify, the total number of her columns is well into the thousands—there are almost 2,300 weekly "Countryside" columns alone, which she and my father started in 1940 and which she continued until about 1982—and thousands more, including the "Penny Pencil" columns and those she wrote for *The Witness, Columbia* magazine, and other publications.

As I stated in the Prologue, my mother and father left me with not only a rich repository of family history, but a priceless archive that has allowed me to reconstruct the lives of two remarkable people and gifted writers who happened to be my parents. This, then, has been their story, and to a lesser extent, mine as well.

Susan Frawley Eisele's "Pocketful of Pencils" column of October 16, 1980, in *The Witness*.

HERE WE ARE well into October with homecomings, reunions, district and regional meetings of all kinds happening, and where to go and where not to go, political wranglings, leaves falling and winter slipping stealthily upon us, all combine to keep us tingling with the very joy of being alive.

* * *

No killing frost or threatening snow have yet come in our area. It will not be necessary to take a trip to the northshore or around Lake Michigan to find beautiful leafage everywhere. Our ancient walnut tree in the back yard is full of golden foliage. Sumac glows firecracker red north of our block about the railroad tracks. Oak trees provide a leathery bower of soft tan. The maples, the high bush cranberries all are putting on a panorama of celestial glory.

* * *

You never miss the water until the well threatens to run dry. Going out early mornings to bring in the daily papers is no longer a ritual. Since the newspaper strike in Minneapolis, getting a slim edition of a paper rates with finding a precious manuscript. For me no other news media can replace it.

* * *

Too much is happening now in my family circle to fully comprehend it. One son flew up from Florida for a short visit with friends and home folks and then flew back on account of he felt a little jittery about his business interests in Palm Beach because of breakins, highjacked planes and getting back safely. My third grandchild arrived here, a little girl, and I have not been able to visit her because of the severe flu going around.

* * *

Which reminds me that some folks make the rounds of the hospital as soon as they hear that someone is there. No matter how serious the condition of the patient is, there is too much visiting going on there. Doctors and hospital personnel try to protect the patient, but common sense should be used by visitors. A card or a call later mean a great deal.

* * *

Auction and rummage sales continue in the area with folks moving out of town or going to work at new jobs by company bus. Old books go well if you deal with a reliable buyer. So does costume or period clothing. I have looked in vain for a large size black top coat with tails. And of course you won't have any trouble selling your old gold and silver. But if you are buying it, you may have to dig down deep into your resources.

* * *

Twice this week while I was out on the boulevard picking up beverage bottles and cans, men drove by on bicycles and they had been bitten by dogs. Cats, too, roam around looking for catnip. Someone could write a book about how careless many American citizens are about disposing of their trash.

* * *

Halloween is right at the doorstep and a good time to indulge in a harmless prank or two. Maybe dress up like a witch, or a ghost.

Suan Frawley Eisele's "Countryside" column of July 8, 1957.

This year of 1957 is said to be the wettest in a century. To be exact, it was in 1858 that the great rains, world-wide did havoc.

The newspapers in this country, in Europe and in Asia commented on the swollen rivers, inundated plains, impassable roads and the lack of sunshine.

"Well, it has cleared up for another shower," became the standing remark.

* * *

Here in our county the spring was late and stormy and the rains incessant. Only the highest ground could be planted and seed rotted in the ground. Creeks became rivers, roads mired down into fathomless mud and bottom lands took on the appearance of permanent lakes. Still it continued to rain. this went on until into July, when it cleared up and the rest of the year was a normal one. But crop damage had been great and the harvest was small.

* * *

A similar pattern followed in 1859, but less widespread, and not as devastating. Two late, wet springs and long, cold characterized the years of 1858-59. then the weather righted itself and fabulous crops were grown.

* * *

Several times this year we have taken the car and on impluse driven out of town into the country, to a roadside park, say, on the river bank, to the farm, over a remote road built on peat beds, through the old lake bed country, across the still virgin stretches of prairie land, in any direction. The longest of these spur-of-the-moment drives have not been more than ten miles in length. Often only half that long.

But each time we have been fortunate enough to come on some enchanting sight. It may have been coincidence. Or it might be some small, sweet, celestial tinkling. This sudden urge must come from somewhere and from someone.

* * *

When Albert was living, he always called us out to see or to hear or to smell or to feel the beauty and the wonder of nature's unfoldings. Maybe he still does. All we know is that we seem to be in the right place at the right time.

For example, early this week we drove out to the farm to baby sit for a few hours while Rose did her stint at the church food stand at the fairgrounds. It's easier to have the grandsons up here for the most part when we baby sit, because of the nature of our work. But this time we decided to go out there. We took a south road instead of the one we usually take. Joe's field of flax was in bloom. To come on your first field of flax in bloom each season is to feel your spirit being crushed in a press, like grapes are pressed for wine. It was at its precise and ultimate moment of glory waiting for us.

* * *

Later this week on our way to Fairmont, we drove, again by impulse, over a mile of little traveled road west of East Chain. Lush, waist-high, ripening grasses rippled like the sea, and made the same sippling sound. Here we found our first milkweed of the year, a colony of it in bloom.

The fencelands and the brush were alive with birds, blue birds, red birds, yellow birds, striped birds and mottled birds. Something had brought them there to congregate. Maybe it was the milkweed in bloom, or perhaps they found a wild raspberry patch. They paid not the slightest notice to our car passing. We drove slowly to watch them more closely.

We have never seen so many different kinds of brightly colored birds assembled together before.

* * *

Does anyone have a recipe for second day cake? We have it somewhere, but can't find it. It has appeared in this column. The cake was served traditionally on the next day after the wedding. A bride-to-be has asked for the recipe. Please send to Susan Frawley Eisele, Blue Earth, Minnesota, Box 365.

* * *

One young girl we know has gone to Omaha for a vacation. She told us that she had made enough to take the trip by baby sitting. "And I'm going to baby sit while I'm there, too!" she added.

* * *

We were at a surprise party not long ago, where the guests did up the dishes afterwards. All of us helped, except one guest. Her mother said, "She is studying for her masters degree, and she shouldn't have to put her hands in a dishpan, do you think?"

Albert's first published short story in *The Catholic World*, June 1937,

DAY OF LEISURE

BY ALBERT EISELE

JAMES McSORLEY had hardly finished the harvest when word came that threshing would begin.

"Good Heaven!" exclaimed James, "nowadays they don't give you time any more between harvesting and threshing to put on clean overalls!"

He was unable to go to church on Sunday, but had to stay home and fix up the hayrack.

On Monday he rose at four o'clock. Dawn was breaking. A shower of rain hung seemingly just behind the grove, but when James walked through the grove and to the edge of it on his way to bring up the cows, he saw that the cloud was far away.

At seven he drove from the yard, waving good-by to his wife and children.

Threshing began at Muller's, three miles distant—at the farther end of the run. The road was a township road, and inch-deep with dust. At each farmstead gate *en route* stood a barking dog.

Threshing, in its opening day, fell almost instantly into its old routine. There was the incessant neighing of strange horses thrown together. John Welke came in with a load of sheaves built wide and squat. John always built his load wide and squat. At dinner the Mullers served rib roast. They always served rib roast to threshers, year after year. The Mullers were prosperous, and the farmplace smelled of tankage, just as it had always smelled.

The Muller job lasted a day and a half, then the machine moved on; to Peterson's, the second of the ten jobs which constituted the run.

The Peterson farmstead was large and heavily wooded, and the machine was set deep in the grove's interior, where no stray breeze could reach and where the fierce July sun beat down without surcease. Threshing chaff floated in the air as though suspended in water.

James McSorley was one of the first teams off the job that second day. He tied his team to a rickety fence, ate his supper, then set out for home. The machine was still running, enveloped with dust and with its blower moaning. The sun had set, and the threshing scene lay clear-cut against the western glow. A faint evening breeze then rose, and the thick threshing dust reached out horizontally over hill and valley, clinging close to the ground like some unified and gaseous serpent and losing itself, at last, upon the gray of the tasseled cornfields.

"The cows were in the corn today," said Mrs. McSorley, when her husband reached home.

"Oh, now we'll have unruly cows to contend with!" said Mr. McSorley, with weariness in his voice.

They threshed all of the following day at Peterson's, finishing late that evening; and on the morning of the fourth day began at Covaleskie's, the third job of the run.

The heat continued, the mercury standing at 105 in the shade. There was a breeze, but it came as from an oven, and the men kept the windmill running, so that fresh drinking water poured constantly from the water-pipe. The water-pipe itself was in the shade of the ivy vines which overclambered the windmill tower; and Grandpa Covaleskie, a sullen old man, kept himself cool by sitting all day on the sweating water-pipe.

Whenever one of the threshers stopped within the vine-enclosed tower to obtain a drink, he was confronted by Grandpa Covaleskie, a clammy figure, who squatted on the water-pipe and blinked hostilely at the intruder.

"Wish we could cool our rumps that way," the threshers said to one another.

On the fifth day the machine moved to the farm of William Allison.

Mr. Allison was a small man physically, but had a voice like a fog horn. His farm was named, appropriately enough, "Echo Hill." Whenever Mr. Allison yelled orders across the yard to his wife, grain trickled from granary knotholes. The farmyard geese never sought to dispute him. His voice, on quiet evenings, could be heard in adjoining townships and came to be accepted, not as the voice of a man but as the voice of a farmstead.

Mr. Allison bawled orders at the threshers all day long, flailing them with his voice and putting their nerves on edge. The heat wave continued apace; sweat ran into the eyes, and even at sundown the heat of the day seemed to linger diabolically in the corners of the fields. Mr. Allison's stock tank was filthy, as it was always filthy, and few of the visiting horses drank; James McSorley's team went waterless throughout the burning day, then that evening drank long and gratefully at the home tank, a disturbed moon dancing in the water to the creaking of the bridle bits.

The following day was Saturday, and some of the younger men talked loudly of "quitting early." But as the day wore on, it became apparent that there would be no early whistle, but that on the contrary the men would work on and finish the job. The Saturday job was the fifth of the run, and the older men thought it would be a fine thing to have the run half-finished by the end of the week.

The men did finish, but the work ran later than expected. James McSorley was the last wagon to go out to the field—he gathered up the final shocks, but darkness had fallen until James had to kneel on the ground in order to detect, on the brow of a hill, the last remaining shocks that stood, like black tents, against the stars beyond.

Early Sunday the McSorleys dashed to church, dashed home again, ate a hurried dinner, then set to work. There were fences to be fixed, granaries to be cleaned out and repaired, and a huge threshing dinner to be planned. The McSorleys would thresh a b o u t Thursday.

M o n d a y morning brought a heavy dew. The men could not load the sheaves till the dew was gone, and by then the day already was stifling and hot, so that the coolness of the early morning hours was lost to work, with nothing remaining but the blazing sun.

James McSorley hauled seven loads of bundles throughout the day, and he was forced at all times to take advantage of every semblance of breeze and shade. On his second load after dinner he was able to work in the protection of a scraggly box-elder, the scant shade of which had moved till it fell upon the threshing machine. He was grateful to the tree.

On Tuesday noon the machine moved to Wampler's. Mr. Wampler lived on a small farm and was a slow and puttery man. He had nothing ready, and the threshing crew had to help him set up his elevator, lock up his pigs and stuff corncobs in granary rat holes.

Even so, they finished Wampler's that day, and began the next morning at Smith's. Mr. Smith farmed four hundred acres, and he had vast flocks and herds. But Mr. Smith farmed too much: he had had no time to haul manure, and there was no place in the yards to set the threshing machine. The disgusted threshermen stepped off, with military strides, distances to south, north, east and west, while loads of sheaves waited on every side. At last the machine was set between two beds of manure, only to have the engine mire itself down. Fence posts were thrust beneath the huge drive wheels until at last the engine was free, but in turn the bundle teams found themselves stuck. There were shouts and curses at the horses, with now and then the dismaying sound of harnesses breaking. The men at last took forks and by hand opened roads through the beds of manure, so that at last the threshing began, but with vile stenches rising from the disturbed manure heaps almost choking the workers.

They worked all day Wednesday at Smith's, and all day Thursday. By Thursday the heat had abated somewhat, but the day was given over to wind and dust. In the afternoon the wind veered, and the belt side became extremely dirty. On the backs of James McSorley's horses the chaff gathered inch-deep like snow; and it broke away in segments when James had finished unloading and drove away from the machine.

No one, throughout the day, could climb off his loaded wagon and lie beneath it in its shade, for the wind drove flurries of dust and chaff across the ground. Along the roadside the sheaves were heavy with traffic dust. At evening the wind died down, but the countryside hung silvery with the dust of hayracks and cars that had passed. For James McSorley there was even, in the moonlight, the dust of cattle that plodded the homeward lane. It was a day of dust, dust that was choking, irritating, ubiquitous.

Friday morning the machine pulled into the McSorley yard. They threshed all day, but did not finish till the middle of Saturday forenoon, when James climbed down from his strawstack, hurried to the house and washed away all that incredible dust and chaff which had plastered his body from head to foot. Then he drew on clean clothes, hitched his horses to the hayrack and hurried after the machine, to take his place at the next and neighboring job.

Sunday came and went, and the third Monday broke again to sunshine and its concomitant threshing.

"I couldn't be sicker of this threshing an' if I had eaten it with a spoon," said James McSorley to his wife as he hitched his team in the morning. "But I think we'll finish to-day—we'll beat the Hanson run, at that."

The Hanson run was an adjoining one, and it would finish at

Mitchell's, a farmplace a quarter of a mile from the McSorley home.

There was smoke in the air on that third Monday. "They're having some bad forest fires in northern Minnesota and in Wisconsin," said the threshers.

The smoke was faint, but occasionally would deepen into a haze; and once James McSorley momentarily failed to recognize his own farmplace, lying soft and unreal in the purple distance.

But the final job was finished that day, and the threshing was done. "Hold your horses!" warned the engineer, and he blew the whistle loud and long.

"I bet you're tired of threshing," said Mrs. McSorley, when her husband came home that night.

"I'm half dead," he replied; "oh, I'm sick of threshing! But I'm going to have a rest—I don't mean to do another lick of work for a week."

He was roused from sleep the next morning by the rattle of hayracks. Guiltily, he rose and went to a window. Two hayracks were going past his home; they belonged to the Hanson run and were on their way to work at Mitchell's, which was a quarter of a mile from the McSorley home.

James McSorley then dressed; his clothes still were wet with the sweat of the previous day.

He b r o u g h t up the cows. Throughout the night the smoke from the forest fires had thickened, and the day now was almost purple. From the Mitchell place could

be heard the sound of the threshing machine, with the moan of its blower falling heavily upon the ear.

James had a late breakfast, and then dallied about till noon, when he ate dinner. "I really didn't earn a dinner to-day," he said.

After dinner he took blankets out on the lawn under a tree, and tried to sleep. But the melancholy moan of the near-by blower kept him awake, and at last he rose, took a fence nippers and began strolling along the pasture fences, pausing now and then to repair a wire. From time to time he glanced toward the Mitchell place; and he could see, through the smoky afternoon, empty hayracks hurrying out to the fields and loaded ones moving slowly in.

The day dragged itself to a welcome close. But over at Mitchell's the machine ran late, its blower sounding its eternal and moaning song.

Then the hayracks began going home. They raised veils of dust which floated integrally away from the highways and hung over the stubble fields, where the work of the day had been.

"My dear," said James McSorley that evening, "to-morrow I'm going to start my fall plowing."

"But James!" said Mrs. McSorley in surprise, "I thought you were going to give yourself a week's vacation?"

"I had intended to," he replied, "but I'm getting sick and tired of this loafing."

The *Commonwheel*, June 1939, "The Brother Who Came" was described by literary magazine editor as "one of the finest short stores ever written."

THE BROTHER WHO CAME

ALBERT EISELE

Albert Eisele is a farmer—just an average farmer, he insists, who rises early for milking and toils with plow and reaper through a fourteen-hour day on his farm near Blue Earth, Minnesota. Yet he finds time to be a poet, a short-story writer, a novelist, a columnist, a husband, and the father of three sons. He contributes a weekly column to the Blue Earth Post, and he and his wife write a joint weekly column on farm life, which appears in twenty-five Iowa and Minnesota papers. His short stories have been published in The Commonweal, The Catholic World, Midland, America, and other magazines, and he is a regular contributor to Spirit.

His art is stark, stripped. What he has to say is truth seen so clearly that it surprises. He writes of the ancient verities. About them clings the odor of the soil.

"Is there any word yet from John? Or from August?" asked Peter Roth again. "The funeral is tomorrow."

There was none, they told him. Immediately at Ottilia's death telegrams had been sent to Peter's three brothers—John, August and Steve. John, the eldest, was a well-to-do shoe merchant in New Jersey. August had prospered on a dairy farm in Wisconsin. Steve lived in South Dakota.

"Of course," said the bereaved husband, "I don't expect Steve to come. He hasn't had a crop in seven years. But I do look for John and August."

"Don't worry, Grandpa," said one of his grandsons; "I'll go right now to the depot and meet the four o'clock train, and somebody may show up."

But the grandson returned alone from the depot. The mild January day drew to a close: the icicles on the farmhouse ceased to lengthen. And by nightfall none of Peter Roth's three brothers had appeared. The house was, however, filled with people from Ottilia's side.

Ottilia had been one of a family of twelve, the stock a virile and teeming one. Ottilia herself, now in her casket at seventy, had borne ten children, all of whom survived her. Grandsons and granddaughters had materialized in such abundance that many of them had grown up almost, as it were, unnoticed—had blossomed one by one and unheralded into young manhood and young womanhood. And now they had all come to the wake, these grandchildren, together with their parents; and together with nieces and nephews of the deceased, and friends, acquaintances and neighbors, in a stream that poured endlessly into the house with all the appearance of people pouring into a public hall.

The farmhouse was a large and modern one, but by eight o'clock it was packed to the doors. By nine a few of the people began leaving, and by ten the crowd had been thinned out by half. And it was also at ten that a car swung into the yard.

The door presently opened, and in came a man, herculean in build, probably in his late fifties and wearing a frayed army overcoat which had insignia on the sleeve. He stood for a moment blinking timidly in the electric light; then Peter Roth came forward and the two men shook hands, fervently and without a word.

Steve was then shown to an inner room, where he knelt for a moment at the bier of his sister-in-law. The two men came away together, and Steve remarked, "Well, she's better off than we are."

"Let me take your coat," said Peter. So Steve gave Peter his army overcoat, frayed and ostensibly (to figure from the time of the World War) in its twentieth year of wear, and Peter bore it away. But the nether-garb disclosed on Steve was also frayed and shabby; and suddenly Steve went to the basement stairway and there descended.

The basement proper was filled with men, while in the furnace room, seated on blocks of firewood, were four others, the remnants of a larger group which had formed there earlier in the evening in overflow from the crowd. Steve peered into this furnace room, then entered and likewise seated himself on a block of wood. Two of the four men were doing the talking, the other two listening.

"The budget this year," said one of the talkers, who held a cigar stub fiercely between his teeth, "is a billion dollars short!" He held the cigar stub exactly in the center of his mouth and his voice issued from all around it in a sort of amphoric or humming effect, much as if a small boy was blowing into an empty bottle.

"A billion short?" exclaimed the second talker, with an incredulous air.

"A billion short!" repeated the first talker. "And that's a lot of money, Joe!" he added, turning to one of the listeners.

"Yes, it is!" agreed the man addressed as Joe; "you bet it is! Yes sir!"

"It's all politics!" the first talker went on. "And as far as I'm concerned, I can't keep politics on the stomach!"

"No, you can't!" said Joe; "you can't do it! No sir. Nope."

"Well," said the second talker, "whether the times get worse or better, I paid the last of my rent yesterday, and now I've got the landlord off my mind for a while, anyway."

"Yes, you have!" said Joe, "you certainly have! Yes sir! Yump. Yump." Joe Weiser was a man who agreed to anything and everything, and as such was an innocent claquer who was always inwardly welcomed by all hands at threshers' meetings, elevator meetings, creamery meetings, co-operative shipping association meetings, and the like.

"I read the other day about what a big thinker said," hummed the man with the cigar stub clenched fiercely in the exact center of his mouth, "and he says, says this big thinker, that what the democrats are trying to do is milk the treasury dry and then whack it over the back with the milk-stool!"

"He's right!" said Joe, "you bet he's right! Don't you think he's right, Emil?" he added, turning to the second listener. But the second listener, as before, merely blinked in silence, being apparently worthless even as a corroborator.

"Rosary!" announced some one at the doorway, at which the five men rose from their blocks of furnace wood and went upstairs.

The rooms ahead were already filled with kneeling figures, so they themselves knelt on the kitchen floor, and from there followed recitation of the Five Joyful Mysteries, led by some unseen person in another room. The devotion completed, the five men returned to the furnace room and to the blocks of cottonwood.

The two talkative ones at once resumed their discourse, and were presently joined by Steve who, seemingly less conscious of his shabby clothes, began to relax and show some signs of life. The men could hear, directly above them, the measured tolling of the kitchen clock. At midnight a lunch was served, and later, at intervals, the group was called upstairs for the Five Sorrowful and the Five Glorious Mysteries. The person who led the rosary was, as before, unseen, and had by this time acquired something of a celestial air.

At early dawn, Steve got his overcoat and went outdoors. The pools that had formed in the fields during the thaw of the day preceding were now frozen over and gleamed under the eastern glow. The countryside itself lay as though just freshly washed. It would be a good day for the funeral.

People began arriving at the farmhouse at an early hour, many bringing parcels of food for the dinner which was to follow the funeral. At halfpast nine it was time to leave for the church; and Peter Roth, the bereaved husband, wept uncontrollably as the

casket was being borne from the home. Outside a woman slipped
and fell, whereupon some one hurriedly sprinkled ashes on the
icy walks. A light wind caught the ash dust and blew it upon the
mourners.

At the church a Solemn Requiem Mass was sung. The church
was crowded: many were old folks who, when the services were
ended, moved slowly and carefully on rubber footing and with
the aid of canes over the slippery walks, at the same time exchang-
ing greetings, in English and in German, with acquaintances
whom they often did not see in months or years.

"The only time we ever get to see each other is at a funeral."

"Nun, wie gehts sonst?"

"O, so langsam und deutlich, Danke."

They laid Ottilia Roth to rest in a newly purchased family plot,
she the first to occupy it, and then her people set out, according to
the custom thereabouts, for the dinner at the Roth home. In the
fields the largest snowdrifts of the winter, now melted down until
the dust-content blacked and streaked them, lay against the slopes
like the skeletons of prehistoric monsters.

The dinner was a large affair. Over a hundred persons were
served. And of these all save one were from Ottilia's side. It was
Steve, Peter's brother from South Dakota, who provided the lone
exception. Steve ate at the first table, together with Peter and the
children. After dinner the brothers sat in an inner room and
talked for a long time. And only once did Peter Roth falter, and
that was when he said, "This dinner reminds me of our wedding
dinner, fifty-two years ago!"

Evening fell, and Peter said, "Steve, you surely need not start
for home tonight. Can't you wait till morning?"

But Steve shook his head. "I'd rather be on my way. If it
should storm, I might be marooned here for weeks. And my car
runs better at night."

Darkness had fallen when Steve was ready to set out for home.
Peter walked with him to the car, and there shook his hand and

bade him good-bye. It was an old car, a coupé, with an extra carburetor lying on the ledge back of the seat.

And then suddenly Peter clasped Steve's shoulders and said, "Steve, I'm so glad you came! You were the only one of my people—" and here Peter broke down and wept.

"Oh, that's all right," said Steve consolingly. "I only wish I could have afforded to bring my whole family. But you know, Peter, I haven't had a crop in seven years! It's drought, and if it isn't drought it's grasshoppers. And you can't do much, you know, when you can't get a crop. I work hard, but it doesn't seem to do much good. You know," and here his voice rose, "it's difficult to get ahead when you do get a crop, but when you have no crop at all, why then, you're just up against it. I tell you, Peter, not to get a crop one year after the other—that isn't right! that isn't right! You're not getting a fair shake—I have to make hay from thistles —I don't understand—" and here Steve in turn broke down and began to weep.

"Now, there!" said Peter, who had recovered himself; "don't worry—things will have to change some time."

"But they don't change!" cried Steve, and his broad shoulders shook as he sobbed like a child. "It's not right when you can't get a crop!—it's not right! it's not right! it isn't fair!"

He recovered himself at last, squared his shoulders, then climbed into the old car and was gone. Peter stood in the yard and watched him go; and when the car had mounted to the brow of a distant rise there was a backfire of the motor that threw out a shawl of sparks. Then the car disappeared below the hill, and only the stars above remained.

This story first appeared in *Ave Maria*, January 1944, and in a 1945 anthology.

The religious experience of a simple man who lived the good life in a simple manner.

FARMER AT FORTY HOURS

BY ALBERT EISELE

Condensed from the Ave Maria*

PETER GREBNER rose at dawn and went to bring in the cows. He felt too tired to tie his shoes; and so he walked with unlaced footgear across the dewy pasture. He felt a sort of disinterested pleasure in the clear November morning. He brought the cows home and milked them, hurried through breakfast, and soon, with his wife and their daughter Mary, was on the way to Mass.

It was Monday, and very unusual for them to be going to Mass on this first of the weekdays, but the Forty Hours was beginning, and the Grebners always made the Forty Hours. Mass was at 6:30, and they were not late. As the sun burst over the clouds, the interior of the church lit up as from a sudden flame. The rays shining through the windows projected patches of color on the opposite wall.

A railingful of people received Holy Communion. These were the ones who had received yesterday. The main body of the parish would go to confession tonight, following the evening services, and they would receive on Tuesday and Wednesday.

*Jan. 1, 1944. Copyright, 1943, by Ave Maria Press.

The priest in charge entered the pulpit. It was not good old Father Finnegan, the pastor, but a strange priest, slight of build, and mild-mannered. He made some announcements, and followed these with a short discourse on Catholic doctrine. The main sermon of the day would be tonight. Soon church was out and the Grebners went home.

Peter Grebner had finished husking his corn, but there was still much other work to be done before winter came. All afternoon he hauled fodder.

In the evening the Grebners went to church again. First there was the Rosary, and then the sermon by the visiting priest. The sermon was scholarly and kindly, but Peter Grebner from where he sat could see four parishioners in familiar sleep. The sermon progressed. Old Grandfather Kissner arose in his pew; Grandmother Kissner, who was sitting beside him, pulled hastily at his coat and he sat down again. Grandfather Kissner was childish, but grandmother always brought him to church with her, and for some reason he was always getting it into his head that Mass was over. He always wanted to go, go, go.

The sermon drew gracefully to a close and Peter Grebner felt grateful, for his feet were beginning to hurt. His Sunday shoes were not exactly new, but they hurt his feet if he wore them too often.

The penitents lined up for confession. There was a long line before both confessionals. In one sat Father Finnegan, in the other the visiting priest. Peter Grebner, for a change, chose the latter.

The confessions went on, with the strange priest hearing them almost as fast as Father Finnegan. That was unusual, for whenever there was a strange confessor, he usually drew the more sorely afflicted. And to shrive the sorely afflicted took somewhat more time, which seemed natural enough. But tonight the strange priest was turning out the goats almost as fast as Father Finnegan was turning out the sheep. And Peter felt grateful for that. For it seemed that the strange priest had a deep understanding of country people who, worn by the day's toil and often with many miles to go, were wont to become physically wearied with standing in line.

At last it was Peter's turn. He found the visiting priest gentle and understanding and pastorly. Peter said his penance, found his wife and daughter waiting, and they went home.

It was a relief to get out of his Sunday shoes. He fell asleep. But it seemed he had been asleep only a minute when his wife woke him, saying, "Peter! Mass is at 6:30; it's time to get up!"

He went out. The tree by the henhouse was white with roosting

Leghorns. The birds caught the gleam of the moon, low in the west and still bright, and they shone like silver. Why did Leghorns always roost in trees? It was November, and time for all chickens to be housed.

He set out for the cows. One of his old shoes had lost its string, and he paused by the strawstack for a sheaf twine. Around the strawstack the frost was heavy and sparkled in the moonlight. Peter selected a twine that had its knot in the exact middle, because no twine knot could be run through the eyelets.

They went to Mass, and received. The visiting priest gave a short homily on Catholic doctrine, but Peter's mind wandered. Catholic doctrine did not bother Peter, what bothered him was getting his pew rent paid and his fall work done. In the afternoon, Peter and his wife worshiped before the Blessed Sacrament from 3:00 to 3:15.

They reached home late in the afternoon, did their chores, and then set out again. "The gas and oil and everything cost us a dollar every time we go to church," Peter complained. His feet hurt, too. Sore feet from Sunday shoes was a sign of a lot of church.

The sermon was like the one on the evening previous, polished and kindly. Chronic sleepers dropped off almost immediately. Grandfather Kissner got up to go; his wife grabbed him by the coat and yanked him down again.

The collection was for the visiting priest. One had to be as generous as possible. But Peter Grebner was pinched for money. He didn't have his pew rent for the year paid yet. He knew that he ought to put in a dollar at least. But he had only a nickel handy, so he put that in. The spiritual riches which one obtained from the Forty Hours couldn't be paid for in silver anyway.

They drove home. The sky clouded over and it was turning colder.

Wednesday was the final day of the Forty Hours, so the Grebners got up early again. It had snowed in the night, a wet snow, one that striped the trunks of the farmstead trees; and the striped trunks leaped into the air as Peter approached with his lantern. In his dilapidated shoes his feet became wet and cold.

They attended Mass. There was the usual short talk, and a brief appearance by Father Finnegan, who said, "Those who have not yet made their contribution for the officiating priest may do so tonight."

"Peter, you made your contribution last night, didn't you?" asked Mrs. Grebner, as they drove home.

"Yes," said Peter. But he did not tell her that he had given only a miserable nickel. "Where is he from, I wonder?"

"From a little place up north, in the drought district," said Mrs. Grebner. "I forget the name of the town, but it is just a small parish, and a poor one, and somebody said that Father Finnegan felt sorry for this priest and had him come here so he could add a dollar or two to his scanty income."

When he had changed clothes, Peter hunted up his four-buckle overshoes. He needed new work shoes, but could not afford them until he sold his hogs. If the sun came out, the light snow would go, and then perhaps the old shoes would do for another week or so.

Peter had a two-wheel trailer. He pumped its tires and ran it to the granary, where he shoveled it full of oats. He hauled the oats to town. It was a small load, but it brought over $7. Now he had a little money. One had to have money to work with.

In the evening the little church was crowded. Everyone had turned out for the closing services of the Forty Hours. Peter was just able to squeeze into his own pew. He left his hat in the aisle, but on second thought brought it inside—one time an awkward boy had squashed it with a genuflection.

Grandfather Kissner was in his pew. During the sermon he arose to go, but his watchful wife jerked him back by his worn coattails.

The sermon ended; the priest left the sanctuary, and the altar boys came out to light the additional candles for Benediction. The collectors appeared. Grandfather Kissner arose once more; his wife yanked him back; and there were those who maintained (those who sat behind him) that Grandfather Kissner was acting entirely normal.

Sometimes Peter had thought that the business of money should not be mixed up with the business of religion. Tonight, however, as he saw the thin visiting priest, he found himself wondering if he got enough to eat. That would be bad, not enough to eat!

Peter took out a dollar bill, folded it a little, and put it in the collection box. That was for the visiting priest. The visiting priest was his own brother in Christ and his brother in poverty.

The Forty Hours came to a close with the hymn *Holy God, We Praise Thy Name*. Peter joined with the singing, though he was never much for singing. But that was such a wonderful song. His eyes misted until all the Benediction tapers had golden lines running up and down from them.

The Commonweal Reader, June 1943.

The Dance

ALBERT EISELE

ALBERT EISELE *of Blue Earth, Minnesota, is a successful farmer, journalist and writer of short stories.*

JIMMY McLANE was eighteen, and his heart was broken. Emma Gales had jilted him. Jimmy had had only one date with Emma, just one. Last Sunday he had taken her to a pleasant evening at the movies. He really was a bashful boy, one whose lips had been kissed only by the wild strawberries that grew in the upland fencerows of his father's farm.

And tonight he was getting ready to play for a dance in the Amber Lake pavilion. A group of players in the town's brass band had organized a six-piece dance orchestra, and Jimmy had been chosen for trombone. Although he had been playing only two years, Jimmy really was a fine trombonist. He played precisely, and he also played the instrument sensibly. He had an innate sense for rhythm and he practiced assiduously: he practiced evenings after supper and when all the chores had been done—in the quiet of the countryside the voice of the trombone carried far, like some huge horn of elfland, and people from the adjoining township sometimes said to Jimmy: "Last night I could hear you play on your trombone."

Of course he didn't feel at all like playing tonight, even if they were playing at the Amber Lake pavilion. This was the most impressive engagement which they had ever had. Up to now they had played only in small dance halls or large barns. But today Jimmy had gotten a letter from Emma saying that she couldn't give him a date next Sunday evening because it was already taken, and all the Sunday nights following were taken, too. "There's a reason!" her letter ended. The reason, Jimmy knew, was Matthew Becker, who had been his erstwhile rival. And now Matthew had won out. Matthew was a neighbor boy, a big, coarse-grained fellow, boastful and noisy; he danced like a horse with one front leg over the neckyoke, but just the same he had won out. A really sensible girl wouldn't have given Matthew a second look. Why did Emma favor him? Maybe she lacked discernment. Maybe she didn't have too much gray matter to go with her blue eyes and her fair skin. Maybe Jimmy had been saved from himself. Well, he probably would forget her in time. But just now it all hurt very much.

Presently a car swung into the yard of the McLane home. It was Billy Grant, the orchestra's violinist and leader, and also the official booking agent. He was on his way to the pavilion, which was some fifteen miles distant, and had stopped to pick up Jimmy.

"The sky doesn't look very good," said Jimmy, nodding toward the northwest.

"I sure hope it doesn't storm!" said Billy. "This is our first chance to play in the pavilion, and we want to make good!"

The setting sun was blanketed with a bank of clouds and flashes of lightning showed far in the background. The fields of oats, fully headed but not yet ripened, shone in the shadowed evening with a bluish sheen.

"How are we playing tonight, on a percentage?" asked Jimmy.

"Right. We get one-third of the gate. We'll make out pretty good, too. Providing it doesn't storm."

"Somebody told me that we got this date only because another orchestra had canceled out. Is that true?"

"I don't know," said Billy. "We got it on short notice, I do know that. But what's the difference—we're playing at the pavilion, aren't we?"

"Yes. It was Joe Kessel who was telling me. He's always the cynic. He said that the other orchestra canceled out because the date was too close after the Fourth. He said that the first dance at the pavilion following the Fourth was never any good, because people were all danced out for about a week after the Fourth."

"Don't worry. We'll have a crowd tonight."

The evening air was motionless, and from the roadside the first katydids could be heard above the motors purr. After the day's intense heat the corn was coming to life and unfurling itself to the utmost: here and there in the gathering darkness individual corn leaves lifted themselves into the air like giant snakes on the alert.

"Gosh, I hope it doesn't storm and spoil everything!" Billy Grant kept repeating.

They turned into the road that skirted the lake and that led to the pavilion. The pavilion was part of a resort assembly that included a bathing beach, picnic grounds, cottages, a rink, a small casino and a ball diamond.

They drew up at the pavilion. The place was deserted. In a few minutes more the other four orchestra members arrived in another car. The six boys then got out and took their instruments inside and put them on the platform. The empty pavilion echoed and re-echoed to the thunderclaps of the approaching storm. The incessant lightning illumined the adjacent lake, the waters of which were becoming choppy with a rising wind that was sweeping away all the sultriness and heat of the earlier day.

The boys coolly ignored the elements and began setting up their paraphernalia. Jimmy oiled his trombone, Eddie Watson arranged his traps and John Haas laid out his various mutes for cornet, placing them within easy reach about his chair and under his music stand. John had a great weakness for mutes. He had about a dozen now, and had ordered six more.

"I'd throw those things away," said Eddie Winston, nodding his head toward the mutes. "Who ever heard of Caruso singing with a carrot in his mouth?"

"I like subdued tones," said John. "I don't like loud noises." A fearful thunderclap seemed to add emphasis to his assertion.

The floor manager appeared, greeted the boys, chatted for a minute, then began dropping some wide barnlike doors down over the screened openings that faced the west and north. Those to the south he left uncovered, and it was just as the storm broke that a car swung into the southern shelter of the pavilion and parked. "Look!" whispered Billy Grant to Jimmy, "—somebody has come to our dance!"

The wind shook the pavilion, the thunder rolled and the rain came down in sheets. There was a smattering of hail, and then the rain slackened, the thunderbolts no longer crackled directly overhead, and at last there were only the flashes of the receding lightning that revealed the pools of water that stood everywhere on the resort grounds.

"About five inches of rain and five hundred rods of lightning!" commented John Haas.

"I'd rather have it five hundred lightning rods," said Eddie Winston.

"Shucks fellows," said Billy Grant, "this'll dry up quicker than a fresh-laid egg and we'll have a crowd yet!"

"This rain'll make the corn come, but not a dance crowd," said Jimmy McLane.

"Crowd or no crowd, we're going to start playing!" said Billy. "The music must always go on, you know. We'll start with number seven. Everybody got it?"

And so the tumult of the elements was supplanted by the tumult of reed and string, brass and concussion. And the music had little more than begun when a couple stepped out on the floor and began to dance. It was Matthew Becker and Emma Gales.

Jimmy McLane, when he saw the couple, dropped one of his trombone notes and played another one flat. So that's whose car it was that had rolled up to the pavilion just before the storm broke! Matthew Becker had followed the orchestra for fifteen miles, and for what? Just so he could flaunt Emma in Jimmy's face! In Jimmy's heart anger now competed with anguish—anger at the thought that this big clodhopper had taken Emma from him, and anguish because—well, anguish because he had lost her. He knew that Emma was not the girl that was meant for him, but nevertheless the anguish was there.

The music paused for a moment; the dancers paused also, and Matthew clapped his big hands together in furious applause while his face gleamed like a plowshare freshly lifted from the furrow to the spring sunlight. The floor manager came up and collected Matthew's ticket. That meant ten cents. The orchestra's share would be one-third. The music struck up again and finished the number, at which Matthew escorted Emma to a seat and then sat down beside her.

This was terrible. This was like playing for a rural wedding dance, where the opening number was always reserved exclusively for the bride and the groom. To Jimmy it seemed that Matthew and Emma were already married, that this was their wedding day and this their wedding dance, and that the triumphant groom had reduced his erstwhile rival to the playing for the dance.

"Number five," announced Billy Grant. And so the orchestra played number five in the dance folio, and again it was a bridal dance, with Emma the bride and Matthew the groom. Jimmy looked at the bridegroom's big feet. Matthew's mother had once told Jimmy's mother that when Matthew was a boy and when button shoes were in vogue he always had to have the buttons set over whenever he got new shoes—"as far over as they'll go," she added. Well, it was a wonder that he didn't have to have special shoes made.

The orchestra played a third number, a fourth, a fifth and a sixth. And always it was a bridal dance for Matthew and his lovely bride. Jimmy prayed for a second couple to appear—any couple, from anywhere. But the floor seemed to exist for Matthew alone. Gradually Jimmy got the idea that there wasn't room for a second couple, that a second couple would spoil the picture: that a dance floor was just like an anvil—on an anvil it was impractical to have more than one blacksmith, on a dance floor it was impractical to have more than one couple.

He asked himself—what did Matthew have that he, Jimmy, didn't? He remembered how on an autumn day both were plowing, each on his father's farm, with the line fence running between them. A large flock of sea gulls appeared and began following Jimmy's plow, where the gulls feasted on the worms and bugs exposed in the new-turned earth. So many gulls there were that they whitened the furrow and filled the air with their exultant and belligerent cries. Suddenly the entire flock flew away and began following Matthew's plow. Jimmy tried desperately to lure the flock back. He set the furrow deeper, that the plow might throw up new and rare bugs and grubs. Flecks of foam began to appear under the harness pads of the laboring horses. But it was the furrow behind Matthew's plow that continued to foam with the gulls; it was the air behind Matthew's furrow that continued to be hung with wings.

Another dance number ended, and now Matthew and Emma left the pavilion and walked toward the casino.

The two stayed in the casino while the orchestra played a number to an empty floor, then they came to their car and went home. And now, to Jimmy, the music had the sound of a threshing machine running empty for the want of sheaves. The other players, too, were beginning to acknowledge the facts. All evening they had played as if to a floor crowded with a hundred couples. But now the bravado was being dropped.

"Let's stop playing and go out and find an orchard," said John Haas. "The harvest apples should be ripe."

"When you play to an empty floor," said Eddie Winston, "you should be blind, and deaf, and have more guts than a packing house."

"It's been a good practice, anyway," said Billy Grant.

They sat there and let the intermission drag on. Then the floor manager appeared: "Sorry, boys, but I guess you struck a bad night. That storm came at just exactly the wrong hour. A storm like that always keeps the crowd away."

"We're taking it as it comes!" said Billy Grant cheerfully.

"There were nine tickets," said the manager. "Ninety cents. That's thirty cents for you boys," and he gave Billy Grant thirty cents. The players packed their instruments and left. The manager switched off the lights, and now the pavilion was dark and deserted.

"Well boys," said Billy Grant, "let's divide the jackpot. Thirty cents— six into thirty goes five times. A nickel apiece!"

"Oh, for gosh sakes keep my nickel!" said Eddie Winston. "Buy music with it, or something!"

"Business is business!" said Billy, and he insisted on dividing the thirty cents, giving each player a nickel. Then they all went home.

And when Jimmy was home he took his nickel, and he placed it under a lamp and looked at it. This coin was a token payment for a lost love. This coin was all that was left from an evening that had weighed so heavily upon his heart. This coin came from Matthew Becker, who had paid, and gladly, for the pleasure of dancing with his bride. Jimmy might have spent this coin for a candy bar, which he could have got there at the casino. He might have choked to death on the candy bar—

252   THE COMMONWEAL READER

a fitting end, to be sure, and a death which would have caused Emma remorse for the rest of her life.

He looked at the coin, and turned it over, and suddenly it became a cynosure and he saw it for what it really was. He bestirred himself and went downstairs and outdoors. Now he knew what to do, and already he was feeling better.

The skies were starry, and there was no sign of the storm of the earlier evening. On the night air was the smell of sweet clover in blossom. In the little pasture not far away he saw the grazing horses move slowly, like ghosts—as the summer advanced the night became more and more ghostly.

Now he crooked his index finger around the nickel and threw the coin, as hard as he could, into the grove. He heard a slight filliping sound among the leaves. . . .

The Catholic World, April 1938 and in the 1943 anthology.

The Farewell Party

ALBERT EISELE

MR. HENRY VOLLMER had sung in the choir for more than thirty years and it was only natural that now, with the Vollmers moving away, the choir members should give him a surprise party.

And this was the night. Mr. Vollmer stood at a window and watched a long line of cars approach along the curving road that led to the farmplace, the cars following one another closely and studding the road with their lights. A lump came into Mr. Vollmer's throat.

"Emma," he said in an unsteady voice. "I'm just afraid that when these good people go home tonight I'll break down and cry like a baby! I always do. Such things get me."

"Well, that's the way the Lord made you, Henry, and you can't help it. And besides, tain't no disgrace for a man to cry."

The choir was composed of eight men. All had brought their wives or sweethearts, and so the Vollmer house was filled. Decks of cards were tossed on tables, and soon everybody was playing progressive five hundred.

"Now, then!" said Mr. Gassonade, the choirmaster, as he seated himself for the second game. He raked in the scattered cards, herded them together and deposited the pack in front of the lady to his right, Mrs. Keene. "Visiting lady deals!" he said politely.

"Oh, dear me!" exclaimed Mrs. Keene, "must I deal?" Her shoulders shuttled and her head wagged.

She dealt the cards gingerly, pausing at intervals to check up and assure herself that all was well. "Have you too many cards?"

From *The Catholic World*, April, 1938. By permission.

—"Oh, what have I done!" She looked to Mr. Vollmer, her partner, for advice and comfort.

And when finally she had decided to play a card she would pass it slowly to the center of the table, hesitate another moment, relinquish her hold on the card and then look at Mr. Vollmer and say, "Oh, I never should have played that!" Mr. Gassonade seldom engaged in side talk while at cards, but during this game he suddenly looked up at Mr. Vollmer and said, "I see by the paper where beer has come back to Kansas after being gone fifty-six years."

"It was gone long enough," said Mr. Vollmer solemnly.

Mr. Vollmer lost this second game, as also he had lost the first. "Oh, you couldn't expect to win, with me for partner!" purled Mrs. Keene in agitation. Her head bobbed and wagged in little bows of apology and regret.

Mr. Gassonade and his partner, victorious, moved on to the next table, Mr. Vollmer remaining but shifting to another seat.

He lost the third game, and also the fourth and fifth. His luck began to draw attention; players at other tables were saying, "Mr. Vollmer hasn't won a game yet!" His fame spread.

He went around and around the table like a horse around an old-fashioned feed grinder. He tried to take his fortunes philosophically; but something, it seemed, had settled in his breast and was beginning to ferment. He tried to console himself with the feeling that he was permanently staged at a fixed point of vantage from where, like the person who stands on a street corner, he could get a good view of things.

Everyone, it seemed, passed before him. There was Mr. Kosmoski, a tenor. Mr. Kosmoski had a fine-timbred voice, very effective on the lower ranges, but inclined to thin out on the upper. Mr. Kosmoski, as an aid, ate peppermint candy — he always had a fresh supply of it, and would pass the bag around and then place it on the organ, where it was open to general foraging.

Opposed to Mr. Kosmoski and his theories was Mr. Hermann, a basso. Mr. Hermann bolstered up his voice with elderberry wine. He carried a bottle with him, and would usually take the necessary swig while ascending the dark stairway that led to the loft. "Nothing tunes up a man's sounding-board like a good drink of elderberry wine," he was fond of saying. Mr. Kosmoski, however, stood his ground, and Sunday after Sunday publicly passed around his peppermints, a tactic which was somehow closed to Mr. Hermann and his bottle.

Mr. Vollmer, in the meantime, had lost the sixth, seventh, and eighth games. His face was red, his mustache bristled, and he was now definitely angry.

And there was Leo Fleming, who had brought his girl with him. The two billed and cooed and tickled each other under the chin. Mr. Vollmer glared at them.

And tenor Philip Kesseling, a good singer and a demon at cards. He played to win; and it was ironical that the two ladies of that ninth game were Mrs. Kosmoski and Mrs. Wetternich, the two most lackadaisical players of the entire gathering. Mrs. Kosmoski played a card and then addressed Mrs. Wetternich: "Did you hear that Lincoln program over the radio the other night?" "No," said Mrs. Wetternich, "I didn't hear it." "It sure was good," Mrs. Kosmoski continued; "it gave everything from the time he was born till he was shot." "Well, for goodness' sakes!" Mrs. Wetternich exclaimed; "and did he live long after he was shot?" "I really couldn't say," replied Mrs. Kosmoski; "there was a lot of music in between, and talking. Is it my play now?"

And Mr. Schmidt, a tenor. Mr. Schmidt was getting old and shaky. He sang by ear, and held a score in his hands merely for the looks of things. It took him a long time to learn his part, but once he learned it he had it. As a card player he was fumbling and inept, the cards falling continually to the table, to his lap, and to the floor. In some strange way he acquired, as the evening wore on, an aura similar to that of the magician who makes cards tumble from armpits and other unseemly places.

It was Mr. Keene, a basso, who opposed Mr. Vollmer at the eleventh game. Mr. Keene was an inveterate latecomer at Mass, and for that matter the choirmaster never bothered much about teaching him the *Kyrie* or even the *Gloria*. But Mr. Keene could play cards, and he gave Mr. Vollmer a fearful walloping. It was Mr. Vollmer's eleventh straight defeat, and he was now boiling inside like a threshing engine.

Then came the twelfth game, the last of the evening. "Everybody keep their seats after this game!" someone announced, this being a promise of sandwiches and coffee.

Mr. Vollmer's partner for this final game was Mrs. Schmidt, and his opponents Mr. Wetternich and Mrs. Hermann. Mrs. Schmidt was a very preoccupied sort of person. She wore strong glasses, which gave her deep-set eyes an oscillating appearance, but her gaze at the same time was fixed and staring. She went seemingly into trances, and when in this condition there was nothing for the other players to do but wait till she came back.

"I have always maintained," she addressed Mr. Vollmer in her slow and measured speech, "that the Catholic Church should make better provisions for its young people to meet one another and become acquainted. A mixed marriage is nothing but a joy and a delight to the devil. The devil is as much a partner to a mixed marriage as is the bridegroom." Her eyes, made manifold by the strong lenses, were on Mr. Vollmer like those of a myriad-orbed apparition.

"A mixed marriage," she went on, lost to the card game, "begins its journey without the blessing of God. There is no Nuptial Mass, and any marriage that is contracted without the blessings of a Nuptial Mass is not a marriage at all, but merely a farce." She moved her head slightly and for a moment her eyes came into focus: they were steady and unblinking like those of an owl. "What we Catholics need are gathering places for our young — study clubs, recreation halls, basket socials, and, under the proper supervision, of course, dances."

All of which was a perennial subject with Mrs. Schmidt. The woman had three unmarried daughters at home, and none of them had a husband in sight. Several desirable young men of the parish had in recent years been married out of the Church, and the villainous injustice of all this loomed so mountainously to the mother that she could hardly understand why public demonstrations did not manifest themselves — she felt that there should be uprisings of the populace; revolution; bloodshed. She brooded intensely over the matter.

She came out of her trance and played her cards. She and Mr. Vollmer won the deal. Mr. Wetternich dealt afresh; the cards shot out from under his hands like grain from an end-gate seeder. Mr. Wetternich was an insurance man, a vapid and blustery fellow who played cards with a vast enthusiasm. He strove always for a noisy table. "You do the playing and I'll run the rake!" he would shout whenever his partner took a trick; and when the opposition won he would exclaim in tones of surprise and dismay, "Oh, oh! Oh, oh! Oh, oh!"

"You got the jump on us," he addressed Mr. Vollmer, "but things'll look different after this next deal. You watch us go! — Oh, boy!" He gathered the cards together and slapped them loudly on the table in front of Mr. Vollmer. "Your deal!" he said, "shoot 'em around!" Mr. Vollmer shuffled the cards and then presented them to Mr. Wetternich to cut; Mr. Wetternich removed the top half of the pack and slapped it to the table with another resounding clap. "Just right!" he beamed; "cut just the way I want 'em! Ha, ha, ha! Now watch my hand! Attaboy!"

He did draw a good hand, and the score was evened. The score then seesawed until the time for the bell drew near. Mr. Vollmer, in what was undoubtedly the final hand of the game, drew a strong run in hearts: he bid eight in the suit, and was not overbid. He had the cards to win, and now if the play could be completed before the bell rang, he would have won a game.

Mr. Vollmer suddenly perked up. For the last hour or two he had been sullenly and bitterly resigned to the bludgeonings of vile fate, but now with the smell of victory in his nostrils he was a new man. He would yet win a game.

But the bell was imminent, and so it was strategy for Mr. Vollmer to rush the playing. He quickly threw away his discards and led. Mrs. Hermann, to his right, played promptly in turn. But Mrs. Schmidt had her gaze on Mr. Vollmer, and she was talking. "We hear so much nowadays as to what is wrong with the world," she said, "but how seldom do people put their finger on the real cause. It is in the mixed marriage that all evil has its root." Her hands were resting on the table, and the cards in them were pushed together in compact form.

"If you will play your cards quickly, Mrs. Schmidt," said Mr. Vollmer, "I think we can still win this game."

"We must bring our young men and our young women together," said Mrs. Schmidt firmly, " — we must take steps in these days and times which it was not necessary to take years ago. It behooves us — "

But here the bell rang, at which Mr. Wetternich bellowed, "We win!" and reaching across the table shook hands violently with his partner, while Mrs. Schmidt turned her head and stared long and studiously in the direction of the ringing, as though she had heard something suspicious.

Refreshments were served, but Mr. Vollmer merely nibbled at his food.

And then came the booby prize — a little fuzzy rabbit that jumped and squeaked when one pressed a rubber bulb attached. Mr. Wetternich, the insurance man, slapped Mr. Vollmer on the back: "We beat him twelve straight! — it shouldn't have been a rabbit at all, but a skunk!"

And presently everybody went home. Mr. Vollmer stood at a window and glared at the disappearing headlights.

"Oh, Henry," spoke Mrs. Vollmer softly, as she laid a hand on her husband's shoulder, "I'm so glad that you didn't break down and cry tonight when the people left!"

America, April 1944.

ALBERT EISELE

Easter Duty

ALBERT EISELE was born on a farm in Iowa, where he grew to manhood. He received his elementary education in a country school and his later training for the combination writing and farming profession which he follows, in home reading and study and in firsthand experience on a modern farm.

Mr. Eisele writes poems and short stories with a semimodern background. In recent years his work has appeared in Spirit, Commonweal, America, *and other magazines.*

Mr. Eisele with his wife, Susan Frawley Eisele, and their three sons lives on a farm near Blue Earth, Minnesota.

---

*H*E LIVED on an eighty-acre farm, and while his farming methods were comparatively those of an Arab plowing with a stick, the farm itself was free of debt and yielded him easily enough to fill his simple needs. Once a week he went to town, which lay two miles away. But beyond this weekly trip for groceries and supplies he went nowhere. He didn't go to church. He didn't go to the movies. He didn't go to neighborhood parties or to annual affairs at the district school. He didn't go to funerals, not even to those concerning his relatives, for he had brothers and sisters living in the community. There was not, to any one's knowledge or even gossip, any bad feeling between the hermit and his brothers and sisters. It was simply that he

150   *MISCELLANEOUS CHARACTERS*

had withdrawn from stranger and kinsman alike, and asked nothing more than to be left alone with his farm and with both his outer and his inner thoughts.

For years now he had been living in seclusion. It was when he was still in his twenties, so the story ran, that he took up his lonely existence, and the story was further that the woman he loved had jilted him at the altar, and that from then on he had looked at neither a woman nor an altar, and indeed at few men. More than one pastor had made an effort to bring him back to the church. "Father," he would say, "I want to keep away from women, and a church is always full of them!"

His neighbors learned to respect his estrangement from the world, but his eccentricities as a farmer were nevertheless obvious and were often the object of amused and even hilarious comment.

First of all there were his irregular hours in the field. Occasionally those hours were standard — to work at seven in the morning, home at twelve, out again at one and home for the day at six. But for the most part he put in but one shift — from about ten in the forenoon until four in the afternoon. Then he would do his chores, have supper, and in busy seasons go out in the evening and work until dark. In August and September, when the heat and the flies were bad for the horses, he would plow during the night, a lantern hung from a lever so that the light shone on the falling furrow, and the lantern moving like a huge glowworm back and forth in the darkness. His habit of plowing during the night was a gesture of indifference toward the sun, but even more so was his more general habit of working over the noon hour. Some of his neighbors did not carry watches but told time by the sun — when one's shadow was straight north and south it was time to go home to dinner. But the hermit's irregular hours seemed to indicate that he had, as far as he was able, excluded even the sun from his life.

His house was unpainted and in a sad state of tumbledown. Many window-panes were stuffed out with rags or replaced by shingles. During a severe blizzard a drift always formed within the house, the drift beginning at the north kitchen window, extending across the kitchen, then through a door and into the dining-room.

He had a mailbox, but he subscribed to no paper and about the only mail he ever got was that sort of matter addressed "Box-holder." He had a car, but it had taken him a long time to get around to buying it. For many years he had made his weekly trip to town with horses and wagon. One mile from the town was the Catholic cemetery, and any car or wagon that chanced to meet a funeral cortège usually halted in respect until the procession had passed. But not so the hermit. If he met a funeral procession he kept right on going. People sometimes wondered about that because, while it was known that he no longer practiced his religion, it was known that his brothers and sisters all were staunch in their Faith and loyalty to the Church — one brother was even a trustee, while another brother and sister sang in the choir. People just couldn't understand how a fallen-away Catholic could be so complete in his dereliction as to refuse to pay respect even to passing dead.

His car, a second-hand one, he bought when he was about fifty years old. This action surprised every one, and it was said that the only reason that he bought the car was because he was becoming famous as "that bachelor who didn't have a car." Of course, notoriety was the last thing he wanted, and the alleged motive for buying the car was possibly verified by the fact that even after he bought the car he went to town only once a week, just as he did before with the horses.

Still another idiosyncrasy, and probably the one on which, with kindly if amused tolerance, the neighbors commented at length and in greatest detail, had to do with a stone in one of the hermit's fields. This stone sat in the center of a ten-acre piece of ground. It was a stone of just such size that the hermit was, by dint of the greatest exertion, able to roll it over. Had the stone been five pounds heavier he could not have handled it. Each spring he seeded or planted up to the very edge of the stone; then he would roll the stone onto the seeded or planted part and go on with his work. In all the succeeding operations, such as disking, harrowing, cultivating or harvesting, he did not molest the stone. Of course, by moving the stone once each spring he was able to harvest perhaps an additional bushel of oats or corn, but nevertheless his neighbors often wondered why, for the sake of an extra bushel or so, he would struggle with that stone in such a manner as to risk bursting a blood vessel. One neighbor offered to come over with tractor and log-chain and drag the stone to the fence-row and out of the way. Another neighbor, who was blasting rock on his own farm, offered to come over and blast the hermit's stone. But the hermit declined their offers. He declined with emphasis. So they said no more about it. He had never given any indications of being a miser or a penny-pincher, so his neighbors dismissed the entire business of the stone as just another quirk.

But if his neighbors dumped the hermit into the hoppers of their daily mills of chitchat, they also did something else — they kept a weather eye on him. He was alone, and there was always the chance of sickness or injury befalling him, with no one to help him or to go for help.

One April day the hermit was seen, as usual each spring, rolling the stone over onto seeded ground. But this time he was seen to struggle with the stone for a long time. Of course, he was getting old; of late years he was aging fast.

His neighbors saw him go home that day early in the afternoon. The day was cool; snow-white gulls were flying about the hermit and his horses, the gulls standing out sharply as they flew low over the dark plowed ground. The next day the weather was warm, but the hermit did not appear in his fields.

"I think I'd better go over there," said Peter Hanson to his wife. "I haven't seen a sign of him for two days."

Hanson went over the first thing in the morning. He found the hermit in bed and ill.

Hanson sent for the hermit's brother, the one who was a trustee of the church. When the brother came, the hermit asked for the priest.

"Father," said the hermit, when the priest arrived, "I'm in poor rig. If it isn't too late . . ." and here he paused.

"Tim," said the priest, "it's never too late in this world."

"I've been away for forty years," said the hermit. "I ought to be ashamed of myself for asking for the Last Sacraments now."

"Tim, you may have been away from the Church, but you never were far away," said the priest. "It is because you never were far away that you are able to come back now. You were never so far away you couldn't hear the steeple bell ring."

"That's right, Father. I could always hear the steeple bell ring. But I never paid any attention to it. It would have been better had I never heard the steeple bell ring."

"Don't be troubled. During all these years you have kept alive the Faith within you."

"Father, I didn't manage this thing right. In some ways I wasn't so bad — in some ways I walked as straight as between two rows of corn. But there's a lot of good things that I didn't do, either. On Sundays, instead of going to Mass, I made hay or dug postholes. I never went to the Sacraments. I never gave a penny to the Church. I even ate meat on Friday. I didn't do a single thing to help keep the Faith in me alive."

"Sometimes it's just as bad the other way," said the priest.

154 MISCELLANEOUS CHARACTERS

"For instance, there are always women who whistle their prayers through their teeth on Sunday, but who for the rest of the week whistle scandal and gossip through their teeth."

"I'm going to die," said the hermit. "I feel it coming on. I'll be gone before morning. I wish I had just ten days to get ready — ten good days, so I could pray all day long. You know, Father, it's just like when the season is late and cold and the corn is ten days late — but ten good and hot days, Father!"

"Yes, I know how it is with corn, Tim. I was born and raised on a farm."

"There was, maybe, one little thing. Maybe I shouldn't even mention it. It's kind of foolish. But just the same — well — "

"Whether or not it is foolish is for God to judge."

"It's no credit to me, Father. It started accidently. You see, it would never have started except that Holy Week comes right in the time of seeding or planting. So I was seeding one afternoon on Holy Saturday. I sowed the oats right up to the stone, and then I says to myself, you used to be a Catholic — why don't you get off your seeding-wagon and roll that stone over? Thinks I, tomorrow is Easter Sunday and the Lord will come forth from His tomb, and there's a stone there in front of His tomb, and maybe the angel that's supposed to roll the stone away will be late or something, or maybe overslept, and our Lord won't be able to come forth when He wants to. And so the thought came to me — I'll just roll away the stone. Not that the Lord was going to rise right here on my farm, of course, but just as a sort of — of a — oh, a memory, that is — "

"Commemoration?" suggested the priest.

"Yes, commemoration, that's the word, Father. I'll roll the stone away as a commemoration, is what I said to myself. So I got off my seeding-wagon that Holy Saturday afternoon and I rolled away the stone — it was heavy, just about all I could handle, and it made me all out of wind, but after I'd rolled it away I felt a whole lot better. And the next year I rolled it away, too, and the year after that, and every year after that. Always in commemoration of our Lord rising from the dead, you see. Last week I rolled it away, on Holy Saturday afternoon, but I guess I overdid myself. I felt something snap inside me. I was able to come home, but I was all done in. I ain't so very ready to go, Father, but I guess I'd better get ready the best I know how. Outside of rolling away the stone every Holy Week, I ain't got no credit coming. I want to receive the Last Sacraments, Father."

"You rolled that stone away for forty years?"

"Yes, Father. But as I said, I don't want no credit for that. It was a silly thing to do."

"It was a beautiful thing to do. It may always have been almost your Easter duty. God will know."

About the Author

Albert Eisele is the founding editor and editor-at-large of *The Hill*, a nonpartisan newspaper covering Congress that he helped start in 1994. His work was submitted for a Pulitzer Prize three times before he stepped down as editor in 2005. His reporting has taken him to more than eighty countries, including covering the war in Iraq in 2005 and 2008.

In 2007, he was Distinguished Visiting Professor at the University of Oklahoma's Gaylord College of Journalism and Mass Communication, and Public Policy Scholar at the Woodrow Wilson International Center for Scholars in Washington, D.C. In 2008, he was the first Resident Scholar of the Eugene McCarthy Center for Public Policy at Saint John's University in Collegeville, Minnesota.

A Washington correspondent for the *St. Paul Dispatch & Pioneer Press* and Knight-Ridder Newspapers from 1965 through 1976, he was press secretary to Vice-President Walter Mondale from 1977 to 1981. In 1982, he was a Fellow of the Institute of Politics at the John F. Kennedy School of Government at Harvard. From 1983 to 1989, he was assistant to William C. Norris, the founder and chairman of Control Data Corp. In 1989, he founded Cornerstone Associates, an international consulting firm and literary agency that brought Soviet President Gorbachev to Minnesota in 1990.

He is the author of an acclaimed dual biography of Eugene McCarthy and Hubert Humphrey, *Almost to the Presidency*, which he is revising and updating, and is writing a biography of the late Cardinal Richard Cushing of Boston. He also contributes to *The Hill* and other magazines and newspapers, and blogs for the *Huffington Post*.

A native of Blue Earth, Minnesota, Eisele is a graduate of Saint John's University and former member of its Board of Regents, and completed two years of pre-medical studies at the University of Minnesota. He was a commissioned officer in the U.S. Army, and a pitcher in the Cleveland Indians baseball farm system. He and his wife have two daughters and live in Falls Church, Virginia.